Plant-Based High-Protein Cookbook

A Complete Vegan Cookbook With Quick and Easy High-Protein Recipes For Bodybuilders

By

Joshua King

Table of Contents

INTRODUCTION 7

CHAPTER 1.   THE BASIC OF PLANT-BASED DIET 11

CHAPTER 2.   WHAT VEGAN IS ALL ABOUT 12

CHAPTER 3.   PRINCIPLES OF BODYBUILDING DIET 14

CHAPTER 4.   MUSCLE GAINS & VEGANISM 20

    POTENTIAL BENEFITS OF THE VEGAN BODYBUILDING DIET 20

CHAPTER 5.   PLANT BASED DIET FOR HEALTH 23

CHAPTER 6.   HIGH PROTEIN DAILY RECIPES 25

    STUFFED AVOCADOS 25

    STUFFED SWEET POTATOES 26

    CAULIFLOWER WITH PEAS 28

    BURGERS WITH MUSHROOM SAUCE 30

    RICE & LENTIL LOAF 33

    CHICKPEAS WITH SWISS CHARD 35

    SPICY BLACK BEANS 37

    MIXED BEAN SOUP 38

    BARLEY & LENTIL STEW 40

CHAPTER 7.   BREAKFAST AND SMOOTHIE RECIPES 43

    CARROTS AND RAISINS MUFFIN 43

    EASY VEGAN TACOS 44

    PORRIDGE WITH OATMEAL AND MACA POWDER 45

    SAVORY POTATO-TURMERIC PANCAKES 46

    SHEER VEGAN MEATZA 47

    SOUR EDAMAME SPREAD 49

    STAMINA TOFU "OMELETTE" 49

    SUPERELAN VEGAN QUARK SMOOTHIE 50

    SWEET POTATO AND ORANGE BREAKFAST BREAD 51

    THE POWER OF BANANA & SOYA SMOOTHIE 53

    VEGAN PARSLEY AND ALMOND BREAD 53

    VEGAN SLOPPY JOE WITH TOFU 55

    VEGAN SUPER GREEN GIANT SMOOTHIE 56

    VEGAN SWEET "FRENCH TOAST" 57

- Spinach and Blueberry Protein Drink 58
- Pick Me Up Coffee Smoothie 59
- Strawberry Vegan Smoothie 60

CHAPTER 8. LUNCH RECIPES 65

- Amazing Potato Dish 65
- Textured Sweet Potatoes and Lentils Delight 66
- Incredibly Tasty Pizza 67
- Rich Beans Soup 69
- Delicious Baked Beans 70
- Indian Lentils 72
- Delicious Butternut Squash Soup 73
- Amazing Mushroom Stew 75
- Simple Tofu Dish 76
- Special Jambalaya 77
- Delicious Chard Soup 79
- Chinese Tofu and Veggies 80
- Wonderful Corn Chowder 82
- Black Eyed Peas Stew 83
- White Bean Cassoulet 85
- Light Jackfruit Dish 87
- Veggie Curry 88

CHAPTER 9. BURGER AND SANDWICHES 90

- Spicy Chickpea Sandwich 90
- Baked Spicy Tofu Sandwich 91
- Lentil Burgers 94
- Sweet Hawaiian Burger 95
- Tofu & Veggie Burgers 97
- Buckwheat Burgers 99

CHAPTER 10. DINNER RECIPES 102

- Green Curry Tofu 102
- African Peanut Protein Stew 104
- Thai Zucchini Noodle Salad 106
- Split Pea and Cauliflower Stew 107
- Black Bean and Pumpkin Chili 109
- Matcha Tofu Soup 111

Sweet Potato Tomato Soup 113
Baked Spicy Tofu Sandwich 114
Vegetable Stir-Fry 117
Creamy Tomato Lentil Soup 119
Chili Carne 121
Mexican Lentil Stew 123
Lentil Meatloaf 125
Black Bean Soup 127
Mushroom Pasta 129
Lemon Pasta Alfredo 130

CHAPTER 11.   DESSERT AND SNACKS 133

Banana-Nut Bread Bars 133
Lemon Coconut Cilantro Rolls 134
Tamari Almonds 135
Tempeh Taco Bites 136
Mushroom Croustades 138
Stuffed Cherry Tomatoes 139
Spicy Black Bean Dip 140
French Onion Pastry Puffs 141
Cheezy Cashew–Roasted Red Pepper Toasts 142
Baked Potato Chips 143
Mushrooms Stuffed With Spinach And Walnuts 145
Salsa Fresca 146
Veggie Hummus Pinwheels 148
Asian Lettuce Rolls 149
Pinto-Pecan Fireballs 150

CHAPTER 12.   PRE-WORKOUT RECIPES 152

Vegan Chili 152
Sweet Potato Meal Bowls 154
Marinated Mushroom Bowls with Wild Rice and Lentils 156
Chirashi Grain Bowl 158
Mushroom Spinach Tofu Wraps 159
Mushroom Pecan Burgers 160
Healthy Vegan Tempeh 162
Broccoli Pesto with Pasta and Cherry Tomatoes 165
Mongolian Meatless Beef 166

    Mexican Lentil Soup 169

CHAPTER 13.   POST-WORKOUT RECIPES 171

    Farro Protein Bowl 171

    Teriyaki Tofu with Quinoa 172

    Buddha Bowl 174

    Chinese Tofu and Broccoli 176

    Peanut Butter Tempeh with Rice 178

    Soy Beans and Puy lentil Salad 180

    Tofu and Greens Stir-Fry with Cashews 181

    Spiced Crusted Tofu with Salad 182

    Sprouts with Green Beans and Nuts 184

    Tofu with Noodles 185

    Black Bean and Seitan Stir-Fry 186

CONCLUSION 189

Introduction

What does it mean to be an athlete, bodybuilder, or any other sports professional? It's about making your active lifestyle the center of your career. It's about pushing yourself further and harder. It's about redefining your limits. To sum it up, your success depends on how you cook, what you eat, how you train, and everything in between. It realizes that who you are is defined by what you do. Athletes have the same number of hours in a day as everyone else.

However, that isn't enough. They need to make the most of every minute to stay on top of the game. You need to make time to eat three meals a day and fit in pre-workout and post-workout snacks. You need to work out to keep in shape and manage your weight. There are hours of training involved. Some games will lead up to competitions, tournaments, and championships.

You'll need time for your muscles to recover. Most importantly, you'll need a good night's sleep. These are essential to overall health as well as wellness.

How does a fitness enthusiast juggle it all? You'll need self-discipline. You'll need to work hard. But what does that have to do with the diet?

There is a saying that goes, "You are what you eat." That means that proper nutrition is crucial to be a good athlete. Which foods make for the strongest and healthiest individuals? Plant-based diets can provide a sports professional with all the protein, carbohydrates, and monosaturated fats they need to reach their full potential. That is because fruits and vegetables, legumes, nuts, and seeds are rich in nutrients, vitamins, minerals, and amino acids. More and more athletes are embracing veganism and are leading their best lives. That is because, after eating protein that comes from plants, sports professionals say they feel more energized and healthier emotionally, physically, and mentally. We'll read up more on that later.

This book does more than promote a vegan lifestyle. It will also guide you in making healthier food choices. The plant-based recipes featured here are high in protein. They taste great and will keep you feeling full. In addition to this, you will learn why it is essential to eat three meals a day and when is the best time to eat them. The recipes also provide background information on some of its' main ingredients. This is because it is good to know what we are putting into our bodies. We hope that with this additional information, you'll be confident that a plant-based diet will ensure optimal functionality for your body and brain.

Dieters and people trying to lose weight are not the only ones who get hit by a new type dieting that comes each year. With so many suggestions like low-fat, low-carb, gluten-free, etc., you just can't decide if you need to focus only on protein or on a whole new diet plan.

I understand your problem; I was in your shoes once. Since I was always changing my diet, lasting results were hard to get. I was going months before I could see new muscles building up. The problem was that my body got confused and didn't know how to configure itself to take the essential nutrients and proteins it needed to stay healthy and still build muscles.

Chapter 1.   The Basic Of Plant-Based Diet

A plant-based diet is widely known for its obvious health advantages, and it has been tried and tested by people from all walks of life. Since it is a meat and dairy-free diet, there are those who assume it to be a low-protein diet—and that's where most of us are wrong. A plant-based diet can be a high-protein diet when consumed with the right approach and understanding. Such awareness is important for people building their muscles or who are involved in athletic activities, as they are the ones who need protein the most for the strengthening of their muscles. In this cookbook, we shall not only discuss the plant-based diet, but it is written with the purpose of providing a high-protein diet to the vegan bodybuilders and athletes. There are several plant-based sources that can be coupled with some plant-based supplements to meet the daily protein needs of a person.

To start with, let's get a clear view of the plant-based diet. This diet, though widely popular, is often confused with a vegetarian diet. The concept is to avoid all animal-sourced food products and rely completely on plant produce. The reasons can vary for each individual. Some may opt for a plant-based diet for its health benefits; others may want to adopt it to save animals—while few others may do so for both such reasons.

What constitutes a plant-based diet? By plant-sourced food, we mean all variety of vegetables, fruits, grains, legumes, lentils, plant oils, seeds, nuts, plant-based milk, grain flours, and vegan cheeses and milk. These products—or the food Prepared purely from them—is referred to as vegan or plant-based. In this list, we find that not a single ingredient is purely protein-based. While protein is largely present in most of the plant-sourced products, it is coupled with other macro and micronutrients as well. For athletes and bodybuilders, the concern is how to consume such products while balancing the proportion of these nutrients in the interest of their muscle building. And that concern leads us to the plant-based, vegan bodybuilding diet.

Chapter 2.   What Vegan Is All About

A lot of people are doing it; a lot of individuals are talking about it, however, there is still a lot of confusion about what a whole food plant-based diet plan implies. Since we break food into its macronutrients: fats, proteins, and carbohydrates; many of us get confused about how to eat.

Whole foods are unprocessed foods that come from the earth. Now, we do consume some minimally processed foods on a whole foods plant-based diet such as entire bread, whole wheat pasta, tofu, non-dairy milk, and some nuts and seed butter the various categories: Whole grains Legumes (generally lentils and beans).

Fruits and veggies Nuts and seeds (including nut butter) Herbs and spices All the above-mentioned classifications make up the entire food plant-based diet. As long as you are eating foods like these regularly, you can forget about carbs, protein, and fat permanently.

Well, the appeal of a whole food plant-based diet plan is that if you don't like a particular food, like in this case, soy, then you do not have to consume it. It is not an essential element in an entire food plant-based diet instead of oats, quinoa instead of wheat; I'm sure you catch the drift now. It does not matter. Simply discover something that fits you.

Even if you have decided to embrace a plant-based diet plan way of life, it does not indicate that is a healthy diet plan. Plant-based diets have their fair share of scrap and other unhealthy eats; case and point, routine intake of vegetable pizzas and non-dairy ice cream. Staying healthy requires you to eat healthy foods-- even within a plant-based diet plan setting.

What to Look Out For When Adopting this Lifestyle

For a lot of people seeking to go plant-based, protein is always a significant concern. There is this idea that's perpetuated by the mainstream media backed by huge meat manufacturers that protein is just found in meat. Well, that's just not true. Standard staples such as nuts, beans, oats, and wild rice included a great deal of protein.

The fact is that foods like kale, broccoli, and almonds include lots of calcium. It's certainly from the greens they eat.

The major issue for a lot of plant-based diet plan followers is typically vitamin B12. B12, for everyone, is normally found in strengthened products, particularly cereals and plant-based milk.

You can adopt a healthy plant-based way of life by basing your diet around Prepared and raw foods filled with leafy and colorful veggies. These will provide your body with the minerals, vitamins, and antioxidants it requires.

Chapter 3.   Principles Of Bodybuilding Diet

Bodybuilding is categorized into three components. Within those three, are detailed steps into acquiring success into a phenomenal physique.

Step 1 : Diet & Nutrition

Bodybuilding is 80% diet and 20% lifting weights. Yes, it's true. What you take in, will result in the outcome of your physical well-being. There are a lot of myths and advertisements that emphasize protein drinks, creatine, pre-work out, etc,. Truth is, none of them are necessary in acquiring muscle and mass. They definitely do help, but like I explained they are not necessary. You can get all your energy, recovery, and mass from the right types of food. In fact, all those supplements that the majority of bodybuilders intake is actually harming your body.

Carbohydrates

Carbohydrates is an important nutrition that creates energy. They are split into three main categories: sugars, starches, and fiber. Most of the carbs in your diet into glucose, which provides energy. They are also turned into fats, which are saved till later use. Eating carbs in the morning will give you the energy to take on the day, and give you strength when training. The goal is to keep a balance in the intake of carbs. Distinguishing between good and bad carbs are vital to your energy and growing muscle.

Vitamins

Vitamins are also very important in bodybuilding and simply taking care of your health. From forming healthy teeth and bones, to maintaining brain function, there are many types of vitamins that help with bodybuilding and recovery.

Calcium

Not only does it help with promoting strong bones and teeth, it is essential for energy metabolism.

Foods that contain Calcium are almonds, cheese, seeds, and yogurts.

Biotin

Turns carbohydrates, protein, and fats into energy.

Foods that contain Biotin are peanut butter, eggs, almonds, and oats.

Iron

Iron transforms the oxygen from your lungs to your muscles and is vital to maintaining energy levels at its highest

Foods that contain Iron are bran cereals, beans, sardines, tofu, spinach, and whole wheat bread.

Vitamin C

Helps turn carbs into fuel and energy.

Foods that contain Vitamin C are broccoli, green and red peppers, brussels sprouts, cauliflower, and spinach.

Vitamin D

Helps absorb calcium, which is essential for muscle contractions.

Foods that contain Vitamin D are eggs, meat, milk, salmon, and fish such as sardines.

Vitamin B12

Vitamin B12 helps form red blood cells, and converts food into energy. It also helps the brain and muscles to communicate effectively resulting in coordination and muscle growth.

Foods that contain Vitamin B12 are eggs, meat, milk, and cheese.

Copper

Copper helps strengthen the tendon tendons needed to lift weights.

Foods that contain Copper are peanuts, crabs and lobsters, seeds, and dark chocolate.

Protein

Protein should be about half of your diet program. It helps oxygen flow through your body as well as building and repairing muscle tissues. Protein, when combined with intense training, help people add muscle mass or simply maintain. They are essentially used to recover from a work-out. Protein powders are popular amongst the bodybuilding crowd as it is easily accessible and helps grow muscles.

These three nutrition, when combined with your weightlifting, will bring significant results. As your body has all of the attributes that these foods and diets have, it is necessary to take in foods that are rich in carbohydrates, vitamins, and protein. Especially, protein. You can obtain all the right essential needs for a great bodybuilding diet from these foods listed above.

Step 2 : Training Plan

Now there are a lot of ways to approach your training plan. An important tool to get you going and to keep you consistent is to create a plan. Schedule a time when you will go to the gym and for how long. Setting a plan and goal daily will keep you to become consistent. Determine how many days a week you will take a rest, as rest is essential to growth. Then, create a plan in which muscle groups you will focus on Day 1, Day 2, and Day 3, so on and so forth. For example, as soon as I wake up, I eat breakfast and head straight to the gym. I then, determine which muscle group I am going to focus on and head straight towards the machine/equipment that are free weights. Free weights are weights such as the bench press, dumb bells, and barbells.

The best way to approach a work out is to start off with free weights. The free weights should work out the muscle group you are focusing on in the biggest and hardest way possible. One warm-up set should be plenty. After about 5-10 sets, go to another free weight for another 5 sets, give or take a few. After about 10 - 15 sets of free weights, go to a machine with a cable that will give your muscle group resistance. After about 2 exercises for about 5 -7 sets each, work on another exercise that will work out the small muscle groups within that muscle groups.

The repetition in each set should be according to the amount of weight you are lifting. When starting off for the first time, or getting back to training from a long break, it is important to form the core of the muscle group first. Start off with low weights, about 60% of what you could actually lift. The repetition goal should be 20 reps and up. Remember, this is just building the core of the muscle, when you are just starting off. This will bring significant results in the first month of your training, maybe less. Sam, a person I was training used this method and he was shocked at how much he improved in a month. He was able to bench press one plate, equal to 135 lbs for about 6-7 reps. Using this method, he put on 25lbs on each side equivalent to 95lbs, and did 20 reps each set for a week and a half. At the end of the week and a half, he was able to hit 30 reps non-stop. He then moved up to 35lbs on each side in the 2nd week equaling in 115bs. He did this for 2 weeks. After the 1st month was done, his bench press improved drastically. He was about to lift 165lbs, on the bench press machine for 2-3 reps. He was able to lift one plate(135lbs.) 10-12 reps easily.

It is not the amount of weight you can lift but the form and consistent improvement. In 2 months after following this method, Sam upped his weights and now went into the regular weight and regular repetition amount. The regular amount should be the weight able to lift in a repetition of 6-8. Even 10 repetition would be good. In the 6th month of training, Sam was now lifting heavily in an average repetition of 6. I have trained him for a year. Within that year, the diet plan, training plan, and rest plan I provided him with brought staggering results.

This method of training is the most basic type of bodybuilding. As you further your improvement in strength, knowledge, and endurance in your road to bodybuilding success, there are different ways you can approach your work out. Now the most important part of bodybuilding is rest.

Step 3 : Rest

Taking on the right approach to your diet, and putting in consistent levels of weight training, your body needs to replenish and refuel. This is when rest comes in. Growth comes from rest. Your body gains muscle, strength, and mass, in the period of sleeping and resting. When my father was training for his bodybuilding competitions, he would work out twice a day for a total of 5 hours. In between his work outs he would take power naps. Naps consisting of about 20 - 40 minutes of sleep. Society today are embedded with the concept of working hard and taking no days off. This will bring you above average results. Your goal is to work smarter, and bring exceptional results. 2 days a week of rest and 5 days of training is a good method. However, the method that I use brought me results that will change a person's physique significantly. For 10 days in a row, I work out every single day, and in those 10 days 4-5 I will go twice. Once in the morning and once in the evening. Your goal is to work out to the point where your muscle group will be almost torn. Vigorously working out, with high intensity training, and then for the next 2 -3 days I would rest. This will allow your muscles to grow exponentially and give you time to refuel. Afterwards, repeat the method. Your goal is to work out to the point where your muscles feel like it is almost tearing, and then rest. The number of days can be altered varying on the person's schedule, but this is how I do it, and it worked wonderfully for me. I like to add some cardio, such as running, or swimming throughout the 10 days to keep my stamina and endurance balanced.

Bodybuilding is a long term commitment of consistency and how much a person is willing to put in. The more you put in, the better your results will be. Bodybuilding helps you mentally, and it is a path that can you bring you success, not only in your physical state, but your work and your personal growth.

Chapter 4. Muscle Gains & Veganism

Every bodybuilder, irrespective of gender, strives to build a strong musculature through heavy training and intensive resistance exercises. And mere exercises can't make much of a difference when there isn't a good diet to support the body changes. Nutrients play a major role in muscle development, and the role of both the macro and the micronutrients cannot be overlooked. Experts believe that for optimal muscle development, about 0.7–1 gram of protein per pound of body weight per day is essential to consume. Keep these values in mind while we make a case for our high protein vegan diet. A bodybuilder must also have a 20% surplus of caloric intake for building and strengthening muscles.

The rise of the plant-based diet has also attracted many athletes and bodybuilders, but many have been skeptical and hesitant to opt for this approach as they were not aware of how a plant-based diet can also be a good source of protein and calories.

This particular concern of bodybuilders led many health experts and nutritionists to work extensively on the vegan diet and create high-protein recipes and develop a dietary approach which can specifically meet the needs of the people who are working for muscle gain. Where most people can simply rely on vegetables, fruits, grains, etc., to meet their energy needs, athletes should look into the diet very carefully and manage the high-protein to carb ratio while maintaining the intake of micronutrients and trace minerals. In a nutshell, a vegan bodybuilding diet is entirely different from a basic plant-based diet, as it is targeted to meet the need of building muscles.

Potential Benefits of the Vegan Bodybuilding Diet

Besides high-protein plant-based alternatives, this diet can provide several other health benefits to a bodybuilder. Let see how this diet can beat the negative effects of a non-vegan dietary approach and how well it can turn out to be for all those who are struggling to gain physical fitness.

Reduces heart disease risk

People consuming animal meat and fats are at more risk of developing heart diseases. The problem basically starts with bad cholesterol, also known as low-density lipoproteins. LDL is largely present in animal or saturated fats and it has the tendency to deposit into the blood vessels. The LDL is present in some amount in all the animal products from meat to dairy. A diet rich in those products can increase the LDL intake which consequently causes heart problems due to obstruction of blood vessels.

The vegan diet provides alternative cholesterol known as high-density lipoproteins, the good cholesterol which can bind the LDL with itself and removes it out of the blood. It does not deposit into the blood vessels and prevents several heart diseases.

Can promote a healthy body weight

For bodybuilders and athletes, there is a constant strive for an ideal or healthy body weight. When the vegan diet is compared to any traditional diet, the results clearly show how well it helps in maintaining body mass index. The plant-based diet does not add up to the body fats. For zero-fat body weight, the vegan diet seems idea for the physical fitness of every person involved in athletic activities. Since it can maintain body weight, it also keeps the problems of insulin resistance and low metabolic activities away from the person.

Protects against certain cancers

Nearly everyone vulnerable to cancer, or the ones suffering from the early stages of it, are prescribed the plant-based diet. There are many features of this diet that can prevent or treat the negative effects of cancer. Firstly, the plants with their phytonutrients have a therapeutic tendency and heal the cellular mutation that can cause cancer. Moreover, this diet makes the body resistant and strong towards the deleterious effects of cancer.

Chapter 5.   Plant Based Diet For Health

Dr. David C Nieman, the director of the Human Performance Laboratory at Appalachia State University in North Carolina, has studied the effects of diet on athletes and their fitness. His subject of study focused on physical fitness and its association with a plant-based or vegan diet.

Dr. Nieman is himself a marathon runner and happens to be a vegetarian. It was his personal interest to learn more about the effects of a vegan diet. According to him, the vegan diet can only prove healthy for the people who are involved in extreme physical exercises and remain engaged in such activities for more than an hour. He suggests a high-protein, low-carb vegan diet to control carb intake. In this way, a person can gain more muscle endurance and improvement in overall body shape and size.

There are also other studies that correlate the vegan diet and physical performance of a person. However, the work in this area is limited so far. However, there are many examples to look up to for inspiration. There are plenty of bodybuilders out there who are vegan and still manage to maintain an ideal body mass index, excellent muscle shape, and a great size.

Torre Washington is a good example. He has practically never tasted meat in his life but no one can guess that with the looks of his muscles and body shape. He was raised in a vegetarian family and grew up eating all kinds of plant-based food. Today he is a certified coach at the National Academy of Sports Medicine and a professional bodybuilder and a sprinter. He switched to veganism about twenty years ago, and he has become a vegan bodybuilding champion though his tailored vegan diet. Torre is a living example of how a vegan diet can best support muscle growth.

Nimai Delgado is another example that comes to mind when we discuss veganism and bodybuilding. Nimai has won the Fresno classic USA championships, Sacramento Pro, Hawaii Pro, and Grand Prix due to his well-maintained physique.

He is now a professional bodybuilder and athlete. He was also a vegetarian from early childhood, and later switched to a 95% vegan diet back in 2015. His muscle shape and size are good enough to give a befitting response to all the critics of the vegan bodybuilding diet.

Patrik Baboumian, an Armenian-German athlete, has also proved the power of plant protein through his great shape and rock-solid muscles. Patrik has been using a vegan diet for the last five years of his twenty-three-year career. And today he feels stronger than ever before. He is quite vocal about the benefits of a vegan diet for bodybuilding and he also uses his social media accounts to debunk all the myths around veganism.

Chapter 6.   High Protein Daily Recipes

Stuffed Avocados

Preparation time: 15 minutes

Servings: 2

Ingredients

1 large avocado, halved and pitted

1 cup cooked chickpeas

¼ cup walnuts, chopped

¼ cup celery stalks, chopped

1 scallion (green part), sliced

1 small garlic clove, minced

1½ tablespoons fresh lemon juice

½ teaspoon olive oil

Salt and ground black pepper, to taste

1 tablespoon sunflower seeds

1 tablespoon fresh cilantro, chopped

How to Prepare

With a spoon, scoop out the flesh from each avocado half.

Then, cut half of the avocado flesh in equal-sized cubes.

In a large bowl, add avocado cubes and remaining ingredients except for sunflower seeds and cilantro and toss to coat well.

Stuff each avocado half with chickpeas mixture evenly.

Serve immediately with the garnishing of sunflower seeds and cilantro.

Nutrition Calories 440

Total Fat 32.2 g Saturated Fat 5 g

Cholesterol 0 mg Sodium 428 mg

Total Carbs 30.2 g Fiber 14.4 g

Sugar 2.3 g Protein 12.6 g

Stuffed Sweet Potatoes

Preparation time: 20 minutes

Cooking time: 40 minutes

Total time: 1 hour

Servings: 2

Ingredients

Sweet Potatoes

1 large sweet potato, halved

½ tablespoon olive oil

Salt and ground black pepper, to taste

Filling

½ tablespoon olive oil

1/3 cup canned chickpeas, rinsed and drained

1 teaspoon curry powder

1/8 teaspoon garlic powder

1/3 cup cooked quinoa

Salt and ground black pepper, to taste

1 teaspoon fresh lime juice

1 teaspoon fresh cilantro, chopped

1 teaspoon sesame seeds

How to Prepare

Preheat the oven to 375°F.

Rub each sweet potato half with oil evenly.

Arrange the sweet potato halves onto a baking sheet, cut-side down, and sprinkle with salt and black pepper.

Bake for 40 minutes, or until sweet potato becomes tender.

Meanwhile, for filling: in a skillet, heat the oil over medium heat and cook the chickpeas, curry powder, and garlic powder for about 6–8 minutes, stirring frequently.

Stir in the cooked quinoa, salt, and black pepper, and remove from the heat.

Remove from the oven and arrange each sweet potato halves onto a plate.

With a fork, fluff the flesh of each half slightly.

Place chickpea mixture in each half and drizzle with lime juice

Serve immediately with the garnishing of cilantro and sesame seeds.

Nutrition

Calories 340

Total Fat 8.2 g

Saturated Fat 1.1 g

Cholesterol 0 mg

Sodium 117 mg

Total Carbs 50 g

Fiber 10 g

Sugar 8.8 g

Protein 12.6 g

Cauliflower with Peas

Preparation time: 15 minutes

Cooking time: 15 minutes

Servings: 3

Ingredients

2 medium tomatoes, chopped

¼ cup water

2 tablespoons olive oil

3 garlic cloves, minced

½ tablespoon fresh ginger, minced

1 teaspoon ground cumin

2 teaspoons ground coriander

1 teaspoon cayenne pepper

¼ teaspoon ground turmeric

2 cups cauliflower, chopped

1 cup fresh green peas, shelled

Salt and ground black pepper, to taste

½ cup warm water

How to Prepare

In a blender, add tomato and ¼ cup of water and pulse until a smooth puree forms. Set aside.

In a large skillet, heat the oil over medium heat and sauté the garlic, ginger, green chilies, and spices for about 1 minute.

Add the cauliflower, peas, and tomato puree and cook, stirring for about 3–4 minutes.

Add the warm water and bring to a boil.

Reduce the heat to medium-low and cook, covered for about 8–10 minutes or until vegetables are done completely. Serve hot.

Nutrition Calories 163

Total Fat 10.1 g Saturated Fat 1.5 g

Cholesterol 0 mg Sodium 79 mg

Total Carbs 16.1 g Fiber 5.6 g

Sugar 6.7 g Protein 6 g

Burgers with Mushroom Sauce

Preparation time: 25 minutes

Cooking time: 30 minutes

Servings: 2

Ingredients

Patties

½ cup millet, rinsed

1 cup hot water

1 (14-ounce) can chickpeas, rinsed, drained, and mashed roughly

1 carrot, peeled and grated finely

½ of red bell pepper, seeded and chopped

½ of yellow onion, chopped

1 garlic clove, minced

½ tablespoon fresh cilantro, chopped

½ teaspoon curry powder

Salt and ground black pepper, to taste

4 tablespoons chickpea flour

2 tablespoons canola oil

Mushroom Sauce

2 cups unsweetened soymilk

2 tablespoons arrowroot flour

1 tablespoon low-sodium soy sauce

Pinch of ground black pepper

1 teaspoon olive oil

¾ cup fresh button mushrooms, chopped

1 garlic clove, minced

2 tablespoons fresh chives, chopped

How to Prepare

For patties: heat a small non-stick pan over medium heat and toast the millet for about 5 minutes, stirring continuously.

Add the hot water and bring to a rolling boil.

Reduce the heat to low and simmer, covered for about 15 minutes.

Remove from the heat and set aside, covered for about 10 minutes.

Uncover the pan and let the millet cool completely.

After cooling, fluff the millet with a fork.

In a large bowl, add the millet and remaining ingredients (except for chickpea flour and oil) and mix until well combined.

Slowly, add the chickpea flour, 1 tablespoon at a time, and mix well.

Make 4 equal-sized patties from the mixture.

In a non-stick frying pan, heat the oil over medium heat and cook the patties for about 3–4 minutes per side, or until golden-brown.

Meanwhile, for mushroom sauce: in a bowl, add the soymilk, flour, soy sauce, and black pepper and beat until smooth. Set aside.

Heat the oil in a skillet over medium heat and sauté the mushrooms and garlic for about 3 minutes. Stir in the soymilk mixture and cook for about 8 minutes, stirring frequently. Stir in the chives and remove from the heat. Place 2 patties onto each serving plate and top with mushroom sauce. Serve immediately.

Nutrition Calories 713 Total Fat 24.2 g Saturated Fat 2.3 g

Cholesterol 0 mg   Sodium 674 mg Total Carbs 92 g

Fiber 17.1 g Sugar 8.5 g   Protein 29.5 g

Rice & Lentil Loaf

Preparation time: 20 minutes

Cooking time: 1 hour 50 minutes

Total time: 2 hours 10 minutes

Servings: 6

Ingredients

1¾ cups plus 2 tablespoons water, divided

½ cup wild rice

½ cup brown lentils

Salt, to taste

½ teaspoon Italian seasoning

1 medium yellow onion, chopped

1 celery stalk, chopped

6 cremini mushrooms, chopped

4 garlic cloves, minced

¾ cup rolled oats

½ cup walnuts, chopped finely

¾ cup sugar-free ketchup

½ teaspoon red pepper flakes, crushed

1 teaspoon fresh rosemary, minced

2 teaspoons fresh thyme, minced

How to Prepare

In a pan, add 1¾ cups of the water, rice, lentils, salt, and Italian seasoning over medium-high heat and bring to a rolling boil.

Reduce the heat to low and cook, covered for about 45 minutes.

Remove the pan from heat and set aside, covered for at least 10 minutes.

Preheat your oven to 350°F and line a 9x5-inch loaf pan with parchment paper.

In a skillet, heat the remaining water over medium heat and sauté the onion, celery, mushrooms, and garlic for about 4–5 minutes.

Remove from the heat and set aside to cool slightly.

In a large bowl, add the oats, walnuts, ketchup, and fresh herbs and mix until well combined.

Add the rice mixture and vegetable mixture and mix well.

In a blender, add the mixture and pulse until just a chunky mixture forms.

Place the mixture into the Prepared loaf pan evenly.

With a piece of foil, cover the loaf pan and bake for about 40 minutes.

Uncover and bake for 20 minutes more, or until top becomes golden-brown.

Remove from the oven and place the loaf pan onto a wire rack for about 10 minutes.

Carefully, invert the loaf onto a platter.

Cut into desired sized slices and serve.

Nutrition

Calories 254 Total Fat 7.5 g Saturated Fat 0.6 g

Cholesterol 0 mg   Sodium 269 mg Total Carbs 38.6 g

Fiber 8.5 g Sugar 8.9 g   Protein 11.5 g

Chickpeas with Swiss Chard

Preparation time: 15 minutes

Cooking time: 15 minutes

Servings: 4

Ingredients

2 tablespoons olive oil

1 medium yellow onion, chopped

4 garlic cloves, minced

1 teaspoon dried thyme, crushed

1 teaspoon dried oregano, crushed

½ teaspoon paprika

1 cup tomato, chopped finely

2½ cups canned chickpeas, rinsed and drained

5 cups Swiss chard

2 tablespoons water

2 tablespoons fresh lemon juice

Salt and ground black pepper, to taste

3 tablespoons fresh basil, chopped

How to Prepare

Heat the olive oil in a skillet over medium heat and sauté onion for about 6-8 minutes.

Add the garlic, herbs, and paprika and sauté for about 1 minute.

Add the Swiss chard and 2 tablespoons water and cook for about 2-3 minutes.

Add the tomatoes and chickpeas and cook for about 2-3 minutes.

Add in the lemon juice, salt, and black pepper, and remove from the heat.

Serve hot with the garnishing of basil.

Nutrition

Calories 260 Total Fat 8.6 g Saturated Fat 1.1 g

Cholesterol 0 mg Sodium 178 mg Total Carbs 34 g

Fiber 8.6 g Sugar 3.1 g Protein 12 g

Spicy Black Beans

Preparation time: 15 minutes

Cooking time: 1 hour 25 minutes

Total time: 1 hour 40 minutes

Servings: 5

Ingredients

4 cups water

1½ cups dried black beans, soaked for 8 hours and drained

½ teaspoon ground turmeric

3 tablespoons olive oil

1 small red onion, chopped finely

1 green chili, chopped

1 (1-inch) piece fresh ginger, minced

2 garlic cloves, minced

1½ tablespoons ground coriander

1 teaspoon ground cumin

½ teaspoon cayenne pepper

Salt, to taste

2 medium tomatoes, chopped finely

¼ cup coconut cream

½ cup fresh cilantro, chopped

How to Prepare

In a large pan, add water, black beans, and turmeric, and bring to a boil on high heat.

Now, reduce the heat to low and cook, covered for about 1 hour or until desired doneness of beans. Meanwhile, in a skillet, heat the oil over medium heat and sauté the onion for about 4–5 minutes. Add the green chili, ginger, garlic, spices, and salt, and sauté for about 1–2 minutes. Stir in the tomatoes and cook for about 10 minutes, stirring occasionally. Transfer the tomato mixture into the pan with black beans and stir to combine. Reduce the heat to medium-low and cook for about 20–25 minutes. Serve hot with the garnishing of coconut cream and cilantro.

Nutrition   Calories 344   Total Fat 11.9 g   Saturated Fat 3.8 g

Cholesterol 0 mg   Sodium 50 mg   Total Carbs 48.5 g

Fiber 10 g   Sugar 10.8 g   Protein 13.6 g

Mixed Bean Soup

Preparation time: 20 minutes

Cooking time: 45 minutes

Total time: 1 hour 5 minutes

Servings: 12

Ingredients

¼ cup vegetable oil

1 large onion, chopped

1 large sweet potato, peeled and cubed

3 carrots, peeled and chopped

3 celery stalks, chopped

3 garlic cloves, minced

2 teaspoons dried thyme, crushed

1 (4-ounce) can green chilies

2 jalapeño peppers, chopped

1 tablespoon ground cumin

4 large tomatoes, chopped finely

2 (16-ounce) cans great northern beans, rinsed and drained

2 (15¼-ounce) cans red kidney beans, rinsed and drained

1 (15-ounce) can black beans, drained and rinsed

9 cups homemade vegetable broth

1 cup fresh cilantro, chopped

How to Prepare

In a Dutch oven, heat the oil over medium heat and sauté the onion, sweet potato, carrots, and celery for about 6–8 minutes.

Add the garlic, thyme, green chilies, jalapeño peppers, and cumin and sauté for about 1 minute.

Add in the tomatoes and cook for about 2-3 minutes. Add the beans and broth and bring to a boil over medium-high heat. Cover the pan with lid and cook for about 25-30 minutes. Stir in the cilantro and remove from heat. Serve hot.

Nutrition Calories 563

Total Fat 6.8 g Saturated Fat 1.4 g Cholesterol 0 mg Sodium 528 mg

Total Carbs 90 g Fiber 31.5 g Sugar 11 g Protein 32.4 g

Barley & Lentil Stew

Preparation time: 20 minutes

Cooking time: 50 minutes

Total time: 1 hour 10 minutes

Servings: 8

Ingredients

2 tablespoons olive oil

2 carrots, peeled and chopped

1 large red onion, chopped

2 celery stalks, chopped

2 garlic cloves, minced

1 teaspoon ground coriander

2 teaspoons ground cumin

1 teaspoon cayenne pepper

1 cup barley

1 cup red lentils

5 cups tomatoes, chopped finely

5-6 cups homemade vegetable broth

6 cups fresh spinach, torn

Salt and ground black pepper, to taste

How to Prepare

In a large pan, heat the oil over medium heat and sauté the carrots, onion, and celery for about 5 minutes.

Add the garlic and spices and sauté for about 1 minute.

Add the barley, lentils, tomatoes, and broth and bring to a rolling boil.

Reduce the heat to low and simmer, covered for about 40 minutes.

Stir in the spinach, salt, and black pepper, and simmer for about 3-4 minutes.

Serve hot.

Nutrition Calories 264

Total Fat 5.8 g Saturated Fat 1 g Cholesterol 0 mg Sodium 540 mg

Total Carbs 41.1 g   Fiber 14.1 g   Sugar 5.8 g   Protein 14.3 g

Chapter 7.   Breakfast And Smoothie Recipes

Carrots and Raisins Muffin

Servings: 4

Preparation time: 5 minutes

Cooking time: 30 minutes

Ingredients

1 1/4 cup almond flour

1/2 cup whole grain flour (any)

3 Tbsp ground almonds

2 cups carrot, grated

1 1/2 tsp baking soda

2 tsp baking powder

2 tsp cinnamon

1/2 tsp salt

1 tsp apple vinegar

1/2 cup extra-virgin olive oil

2 Tbsp linseed oil

4 Tbsp organic honey

3 oz raisins seedless

Directions:

Preheat oven to 360 F.

In a big bowl, combine together almond flour, whole grain flour, baking soda, baking powder, cinnamon, and salt.

In a separate bowl, whisk apple vinegar, olive oil, linseed oil, and honey.

Combine almond flour mixture with liquid mixture; stir well.

Add in the shredded carrots and raisins; stir well.

Fill the muffin cups 3/4 of the way full.

Bake for 30 minutes.

Remove from the oven, and allow to cool for 10 minutes.

Serve.

Easy Vegan Tacos

Servings: 2

Preparation time: 5 minutes

Cooking time: 10 minutes

Ingredients:

Taco Shells (8)

Corn (.25 C.)

Chopped Cherry Tomatoes (8)

Chopped Avocado (1)

Ground Cumin (2 t.)

Hot Sauce (2 t.)

Tomato Puree (1 C.)

Black Beans (2 C.)

Directions: To begin this recipe, you will want to take a pan and place it over medium heat. As the pan begins to warm up, add in the tomato puree, black beans, hot sauce, and cumin. Cook all of these ingredients together for about five minutes or until everything is warmed through. At this point, feel free to season the dish however you would like. Next, you will begin to assemble the tacos. All you need to do is pour in as much or as little bean mixture into each taco

Porridge with Oatmeal and Maca Powder

Servings: 2

Preparation time: 5 minutes

Cooking time: 10 minutes

Ingredients

2 cups almond milk (or coconut milk) unsweetened

1 pinch of table salt

1 cup rolled oats

1 1/2 Tbsp Maca powder

1 Tbsp honey (or maple syrup)

1 tsp ground cinnamon

1 banana peeled and thinly sliced

Directions: In a saucepan, heat almond milk with a pinch of salt over high heat; bring to boiling. Stir in rolled oats and Maca powder, reduce heat to medium and simmer, uncovered, for 5 to 7 minutes; stir constantly. Place oatmeal in a bowl and pour over the honey, cinnamon, and banana slices. Serve and enjoy!

Savory Potato-Turmeric Pancakes

Servings: 4

Preparation time: 5 minutes

Cooking time: 15 minutes

Ingredients

4 large potatoes, grated

1 tsp of turmeric powder

1 Tbsp almond butter with salt added

Salt and ground pepper to taste

1/2 cup of garlic-infused olive oil

Serving: fresh chopped parsley or sliced green onions

Directions: Peel, wash, and pat dry potatoes. Grate potatoes over a plate or bowl. Season potatoes with the salt and pepper and turmeric.

Heat oil in a large frying skillet over medium-strong heat Spoon grated potatoes into hot oil and press with a spatula. Cook for about 2 minutes; flip the pancake and cook until golden brown. Transfer pancake to the kitchen paper towel. Serve warm with chopped parsley or green onion.

Sheer Vegan Meatza

Servings: 3

Preparation time: 15 minutes

Cooking time: 50 minutes

Ingredients

Cauliflower Crust

1/2 cup avocado oil

1 head cauliflower cut into florets

1/2 tsp garlic minced

Salt and ground pepper to taste

1/2 cup button mushrooms thinly sliced

2 Tbsp arrowroot powder

Filling/topping

1/2 cup of ketchup

1 cup mushrooms sliced

1 cup avocado puree (mashed)

1/2 cup grated carrot

1 cup olives, pitted, sliced or halved

Directions:

Cauliflower dough:

Preheat oven to 400F.

Cover a baking sheet with parchment paper.

Add cauliflower florets into your food processor into batches.

Process cauliflower florets until they achieve a form of rice.

Cook cauliflower in non-stick frying skillet for about 8 to 10 minutes.

Transfer cauliflower rice into a bowl and add mushrooms, ground garlic, arrowroot powder, some oil, and the salt and pepper; stir well.

Spread cauliflower dough onto a prepared baking sheet, and bake for about 20 minutes.

Remove from oven, and allow it to cool for 10 minutes.   Toppings

Fill the dough with ketchup, avocado puree, sliced mushrooms, carrot, and sprinkle with little avocado oil.   Place dough in the oven and bake for 10 to 12 minutes. Slice and serve hot.

Sour Edamame Spread

Servings: 6

Preparation time: 5 minutes

Cooking time: 5 minutes

Ingredients

2 cups frozen unshelled edamame, cooked according to package directions

1/4 cup sesame oil , 1 cup silken tofu, drained

1 Tbsp minced garlic (from 3 medium cloves)

Flaky sea salt to taste

White pepper to taste

2 tsp ground cumin , 1 Tbsp rice vinegar, 4 Tbsp fresh lemon juice

Sesame seeds for serving

Directions: Place all ingredients into your high-speed blender or into a food processor. Blend until combined well. Transfer spread to a bowl and a sprinkle with sesame seeds. Edamame spread can be refrigerated in an airtight container up to 3 days.

Stamina Tofu "Omelette"

Servings: 2

Preparation time: 8 minutes

Cooking time: 12 minutes

Ingredients

2 Tbsp of olive oil

1 small onion finely chopped

1 large red pepper chopped

1/2 cup white mushrooms halved or sliced

3/4 lb tofu cut into cubes, 1 Tbsp nutritional yeast

1 tsp turmeric (for color), 1 tsp of garlic powder

Sea salt and ground black pepper to taste

Directions: Heat oil in a large frying pan over medium-high heat. Sauté onion and red pepper with a pinch of salt for 2 to 3 minutes. Add mushrooms and cook until most of the water from the mushrooms has evaporated. Add tofu cubes and all remaining ingredients; stir well. Cover and cook over medium heat for about 6 to 8 minutes; stir occasionally. Taste and adjust seasonings. Serve hot.

Superelan Vegan Quark Smoothie

Servings: 2

Preparation time: 5 minutes

Cooking time: 5 minutes

Ingredients

1 frozen banana

3/4 cup frozen berries

1 apple cored and sliced

1/3 cup oats

1 scoop vegan protein powder (Soy or Hemp Protein)

3/4 cup vegan quark (for example Alpro)

1 1/2 cups almond milk

Directions:

Place all ingredients into your fast-speed blender.

Blend until smooth and creamy.

Serve immediately.

Sweet Potato and Orange Breakfast Bread

Servings: 6

Preparation time: 5 minutes

Cooking time: 50 minutes

Ingredients

1 large sweet potato (about 12 oz.), peeled and shredded

1/2 cup fresh orange juice

1/3 cup water

1/3 cup orange marmalade

4 Tbsp canola oil

1 Tbsp arrowroot powder

3 cups flour self-rising

1/2 cup sugar

2 tsp baking powder

1/4 tsp salt

Directions:

Preheat oven to 375 F/180 C.

In a small saucepan, cook the shredded sweet potato for 10 min; drain and cool.

In a bowl, combine shredder potato with orange juice, water, orange marmalade, canola oil, and arrowroot powder.

In a separate bowl, combine together the flour, sugar, baking powder, and salt.

Add the liquid ingredients to the flour mixture and stir just until combined.

Spoon batter into greased loaf pan and bake for 30-35 minutes.

When ready, allow it to cool for 10 minutes.

Slice and serve.

The Power of Banana & Soya Smoothie

Servings: 2

Preparation time: 5 minutes

Cooking time: 5 minutes

Ingredients

3/4 cup soya milk

2 bananas frozen

1 kiwi fruit sliced

1 Tbsp hemp seeds

1 Tbsp linseed oil

1 scoop vegan protein powder (pea or soy protein)

1 cup fresh spinach

3/4 cup frozen berries thawed (unsweetened)

Directions:

Place all ingredients in your blender.

Blend for about 45 seconds or until everything is well mixed. Serve.

Vegan Parsley and Almond Bread

Servings: 2

Preparation time: 10 minutes

Cooking time: 1 hour

Ingredients

1 1/2 cups sparkling water on room temperature

1 Tbsp of active dry yeast

1 tsp sugar

3 Tbsp olive oil

2 1/2 cups self-rising flour

2 Tbsp fresh minced parsley

1/2 cup almonds finely chopped

1 tsp ground garlic

1 tsp   salt

Directions:

Preheat oven to 375 F/185 C.

Grease a baking loaf with olive oil; set aside.

In a large bowl, dissolve yeast, sugar, and salt in sparkling water; let stand until bubbles form on the surface.

Add in flour and olive oil and beat until smooth.

Add all remaining ingredients, and continue to beat until combined well or until form soft dough.

Turn onto a floured surface; knead until smooth and elastic or for about 8 minutes.

Shape dough into a loaf, and place into a prepared bread loaf.

Bake for 30 to 35 minutes or until golden brown.

Remove from oven, and let sit for 10 minutes.

Slice, serve, and enjoy!

Vegan Sloppy Joe with Tofu

Servings: 4

Preparation time:

Cooking time:

Ingredients

2 Tbsp avocado oil

1 onion finely sliced

2 cloves garlic finely sliced

1 lb tofu cheese, cubed

1 jalapeno pepper sliced

1 green bell pepper, diced

1 large tomato diced

3 Tbsp tomato paste

2 Tbsp fajita spice mix

Salt and ground black pepper

1 cup of water

Directions:

Heat oil in large frying skillet over medium heat.

Add sliced green onion, garlic, green pepper, and jalapeno pepper; sauté with a pinch of pepper for 3 to 4 minutes or until soft.

Add tofu and brown for a further 3 minutes; stir constantly.

Add diced tomato, tomato paste, water, and fajita spice mix; cover and cook on medium-low heat for 10 minutes.

Taste and adjust salt and pepper to taste.

Serve immediately or keep refrigerated.

Vegan Super Green Giant Smoothie

Servings: 2

Preparation time: 5 minutes

Cooking time: 5 minutes

Ingredients

1 1/2 cups almond milk (or coconut milk)

1 cup of carrot tops chopped

1 cup fresh spinach chopped

1 cucumber, peeled and sliced

1 large banana, fresh or frozen

3 Tbsp ground almonds or ground Macadamia almonds

1 scoop vegan protein powder (pea or soy protein)

1 Tbsp extracted honey

1 Tbsp linseed oil

Directions: Place all ingredients in your fast-speed blender. Blend until smooth and combined well. Serve.

Vegan Sweet "French Toast"

Servings: 2

Preparation time: 5 minutes

Cooking time: 10 minutes

Ingredients

3 Tbsp olive oil

1 cup of soy milk (unsweetened)

1 cup oat flour (or buckwheat)

1/2 tsp cinnamon

2 Tbsp brown sugar or sugar

6 slices day-old bread (or multi-grain bread)

Servings; vegan spread, groundnuts, honey or Maple syrup

Directions:

Heat oil in a frying skillet over medium-high heat.

Pour soy milk in one bowl.

In a separate bowl, combine together oat flakes and brown sugar; stir well.

Dip each bread slice first in soy milk, and then roll into oat flakes mixture.

Fry your vegan French toast for a couple of minutes on each side, or until golden brown.

Remove French toast onto a lined plate with kitchen paper to drain.

Serve with your favorite vegan spread, groundnuts, honey or Maple syrup.

Spinach and Blueberry Protein Drink

Preparation time: 5 Minutes
Cooking time: None
Servings: 2

Ingredients:

½ cup of vegan yogurt

¼ cup of mixed berries

1/3 cup of non-dairy milk

1 cup of leafy greens

1 scoop of vegan protein powder

1/3 cup of ice

Directions:

Add all the ingredients into a food processor, except the ice

Blend until smooth, then add ice

Blend until ice is crushed, then serve

Pick Me Up Coffee Smoothie

Preparation Time: 5 Minutes
Cooking time: None
Servings: 2

Ingredients:

1 can coconut milk

3 frozen bananas

2 tbsp peanut butter

4 tsp instant coffee powder

2 tbsp maple syrup

Directions:

Peel and chop fresh bananas into pieces

Freeze for 2 hours before use

In a food processor, add non-dairy milk, frozen bananas, peanut butter, instant coffee powder and maple syrup

Blend until smooth

Strawberry Vegan Smoothie

Preparation Time: 5 Minutes
Cooking time: None
Servings: 2

Ingredients:

2 cups strawberries

1 banana

1/4 cup non-dairy milk

2 tbsp maple syrup

Directions:

In a food processor, blend strawberries, banana, milk and maple syrup

Pour in two serving glasses and enjoy

Avocado Green Smoothie

Preparation Time: 5 Minutes

Cooking time: None

Servings: 2

Ingredients:

1/2 avocado

1 banana

1 cup spinach

1 cup non-dairy milk

2 pitted dates

Directions:

In a food processor, blend the avocado, banana, spinach, milk and dates until smooth

Pour in two serving glasses and enjoy

Granola Bars

For some additional ideas of pre-workout snacks, consider a granola bar. What is it? The basic recipe contains oats, nuts and seeds and dried fruit. Oats, have fiber. It lowers cholesterol levels and reduces the risk of developing heart diseases.

The ingredients are then held together with maple syrup or agave. They are convenient because they are small and don't need to be kept cold. Since they often come pre-portioned, it prevents over-eating.

This makes it easier to manage weight. Granola bars also taste good and come in a variety of flavors. In terms of health benefits, granola bars can be a good source of fiber and protein, as well. However, just like with protein smoothies, not every granola bar is considered healthy. This is the case when it contains ingredients that can minimize the results of your training efforts.

Yes, granola bars can be a healthy choice for athletes. However, this isn't always the case. We recommend you check the ingredient list of those you buy at the grocery store. That's because artificial ingredients, high levels of sugar and added calories can impede on your fitness goals. They are often highly processed, which may be the cause of developing metabolic syndrome. It is responsible for several health conditions like diabetes, heart disease and a stroke.

Processed foods contain artificial ingredients, which means a consumer can't know with certainty what exactly they are ingesting. In addition to this, some store-bought granola bar brands go over the recommended amount of sugar you should eat in a day. Excess sugar is often the underlying cause of weight gain. If not controlled, this can lead to obesity and diabetes. Some people assume that sugar alcohols are better alternatives to sugar but have their share of problems. For instance, they may not be broken down by your body as effectively.

They may also present adverse effects to those with a sensitivity towards xylitol or sorbitol. Other artificial sweeteners like aspartame, saccharin and sucralose react negatively on one's gut health and make it more difficult for your body to keep blood sugar under control.

Knowing this, you are perhaps asking yourself what you should look for in a granola bar. For it to be healthy, it should be made up of real ingredients. These include grains such as oats, as well as fruit, seed and nuts. Ideally, real foods have ingredients that you can pronounce. Their sugar content should be under 10 grams. For it to be nourishing, it should have over 5 grams of protein. A healthy granola bar should also have a source of fiber, so at least 3 grams. As for the number of calories, it shouldn't exceed 250.

Furthermore, you should know that first impressions matter, when it comes to food. What do we mean by this? Simply put, ingredients are listed in the order they appear in. What the product has the most of will be listed first. Adversely, what the product has least of will be listed last. If sugar features among the granola bar's first three ingredients, then it should be avoided. It is not a healthy snack choice for you.

As a vegan, you must also check the ingredient list to be sure it is 100% plant-based. Because of the hassle, it can be to choose the right granola bar for you and your fitness goals; some people want not to eat them. However, we offer something much more interesting: the option of making your granola bar.

Doing so is inexpensive, as the ingredients are likely to already be in your kitchen pantry. It gives the versatility of adapting the recipe to your personal preferences. It is also a food that you can make in batches and freeze for later. They can be as straightforward or as elaborate as you want them to be. However, to provide your body with the macronutrients it needs to enhance athletic performance, we'll keep this recipe short and sweet.

One of its' key ingredients is hemp, a superfood. It is a good source of omega 3, 6 and 9. It also has magnesium, manganese, iron and zinc. This ingredient is helpful for athletes, as it can help reduce pain in the tendons and ligaments. It also improves oxygen circulate more quickly in the bloodstream. In addition to this, hemp has anti-inflammatory properties, making it a great food to include in an athlete's diet.

Another nutrient-rich ingredient in this recipe is the date. Although this dry fruit has a higher number of calories, its' other health benefits make it an ingredient worth having in your diet. Dates have a low glycemic index. They are high in fiber, which helps digestive health and regulates bowel movement. It also slows digestion, which gives your body a greater control of blood sugar levels.

Dates are also high in antioxidants, which fight to reduce your risk of developing chronic disease. Some of the antioxidants found in dates are flavonoids, carotenoids and phenolic acid. These aid in reducing inflammation and in promoting cardiovascular health. Furthermore, dates are good for the human brain. We must not underestimate the usefulness of the brain in a workout, training and a big game. A healthy brain means improved memory, a better ability to learn and increased alertness. Moreover, dates make great natural sweeteners and can easily replace sugar in a recipe. Often, this is achieved by mixing dates with water to create a paste. If you need more convincing on how good dates are for you, know this. Dates help make for strong bones, too, because of nutrients like calcium, magnesium, phosphorus and potassium. In this instance, dates are being added to your granola bar. It will serve as the binding ingredient that holds your protein bar together. However, the versatility of this fruit makes it a great addition to sauces, salad dressings, marinades and oatmeal, too. In

Chapter 8.   Lunch Recipes

Amazing Potato Dish

Preparation time: 10 minutes

Cooking time: 3 hours

Servings: 4

Ingredients:

1 and ½ pounds potatoes, peeled and roughly chopped

1 tablespoon olive oil

3 tablespoons water

1 small yellow onion, chopped

½ Cup veggie stock cube, crumbled

½ Teaspoon coriander, ground

½ Teaspoon cumin, ground

½ Teaspoon garam masala

½ Teaspoon chili powder

Black pepper to the taste

½ Pound spinach, roughly torn

Directions:

Put the potatoes in your slow cooker.

Add oil, water, onion, stock cube, coriander, cumin, garam masala, chili powder, black pepper and spinach.

Stir, cover and cook on High for 3 hours.

Divide into bowls and serve.

Enjoy!

Nutrition: calories 270, fat 4, fiber 6, carbs 8, protein 12

Textured Sweet Potatoes and Lentils Delight

Preparation time: 10 minutes

Cooking time: 4 hours and 30 minutes

Servings: 6

Ingredients:

6 cups sweet potatoes, peeled and cubed

2 teaspoons coriander, ground

2 teaspoons chili powder

1 yellow onion, chopped

3 cups veggie stock

4 garlic cloves, minced

A pinch of sea salt and black pepper

10 ounces canned coconut milk

1 cup water

1 and ½ cups red lentils

Directions:

Put sweet potatoes in your slow cooker.

Add coriander, chili powder, onion, stock, garlic, salt and pepper, stir, cover and cook on high for 3 hours.

Add lentils, stir, cover and cook for 1 hour and 30 minutes.

Add water and coconut milk, stir well, divide into bowls and serve right away.

Enjoy!

Nutrition: calories 300, fat 10, fiber 8, carbs 16, protein 10

Incredibly Tasty Pizza

Preparation time: 1 hour and 10 minutes

Cooking time: 1 hour and 45 minutes

Servings: 3

Ingredients:

For the dough:

½ Teaspoon italian seasoning

1 and ½ cups whole wheat flour

1 and ½ teaspoons instant yeast

1 tablespoon olive oil

A pinch of salt

½ Cup warm water

Cooking spray

For the sauce:

¼ Cup green olives, pitted and sliced

¼ Cup kalamata olives, pitted and sliced

½ Cup tomatoes, crushed

1 tablespoon parsley, chopped

1 tablespoon capers, rinsed

¼ Teaspoon garlic powder

¼ Teaspoon basil, dried

¼ Teaspoon oregano, dried

¼ Teaspoon palm sugar

¼ Teaspoon red pepper flakes

A pinch of salt and black pepper

½ Cup cashew mozzarella, shredded

Directions:

In your food processor, mix yeast with italian seasoning, a pinch of salt and flour.

Add oil and the water and blend well until you obtain a dough.

Transfer dough to a floured working surface, knead well, transfer to a greased bowl, cover and leave aside for 1 hour.

Meanwhile, in a bowl, mix green olives with kalamata olives, tomatoes, parsley, capers, garlic powder, oregano, sugar, salt, pepper and pepper flakes and stir well.

Transfer pizza dough to a working surface again and flatten it.

Shape so it will fit your slow cooker.

Grease your slow cooker with cooking spray and add dough.

Press well on the bottom.

Spread the sauce mix all over, cover and cook on high for 1 hour and 15 minutes.

Spread vegan mozzarella all over, cover again and cook on high for 30 minutes more.

Leave your pizza to cool down before slicing and serving it.

Nutrition: calories 340, fat 5, fiber 7, carbs 13, protein 15

Rich Beans Soup

Preparation time: 10 minutes

Cooking time: 7 hours

Servings: 4

Ingredients: 1 pound navy beans, 1 yellow onion, chopped

4 garlic cloves, crushed, 2 quarts veggie stock

A pinch of sea salt

Black pepper to the taste

2 potatoes, peeled and cubed

2 teaspoons dill, dried

1 cup sun-dried tomatoes, chopped

1 pound carrots, sliced, 4 tablespoons parsley, minced

Directions: Put the stock in your slow cooker. Add beans, onion, garlic, potatoes, tomatoes, carrots, dill, salt and pepper, stir, cover and cook on low for 7 hours. Stir your soup, add parsley, divide into bowls and serve. Enjoy!

Nutrition: calories 250, fat 4, fiber 3, carbs 9, protein 10

Delicious Baked Beans

Preparation time: 10 minutes

Cooking time: 12 hours

Servings: 8

Ingredients:

1 pound navy beans, soaked overnight and drained

1 cup maple syrup

1 cup bourbon

1 cup vegan bbq sauce

1 cup palm sugar

¼ Cup ketchup

1 cup water

¼ Cup mustard

¼ Cup blackstrap molasses

¼ Cup apple cider vinegar

¼ Cup olive oil

2 tablespoons coconut aminos

Directions:

Put the beans in your slow cooker.

Add maple syrup, bourbon, bbq sauce, sugar, ketchup, water, mustard, molasses, vinegar, oil and coconut aminos.

Stir everything, cover and cook on Low for 12 hours.

Divide into bowls and serve.

Enjoy!

Nutrition: calories 430, fat 7, fiber 8, carbs 15, protein 19

Indian Lentils

Preparation time: 10 minutes

Cooking time: 3 hours

Servings: 4

Ingredients:

1 yellow bell pepper, chopped

1 sweet potato, chopped

2 and ½ cups lentils, already cooked

4 garlic cloves, minced

1 yellow onion, chopped

2 teaspoons cumin, ground

15 ounces canned tomato sauce

½ Teaspoon ginger, ground

A pinch of cayenne pepper

1 tablespoons coriander, ground

1 teaspoon turmeric, ground

2 teaspoons paprika

2/3 cup veggie stock

1 teaspoon garam masala

A pinch of sea salt

Black pepper to the taste

Juice of 1 lemon

Directions:

Put the stock in your slow cooker.

Add potato, lentils, onion, garlic, cumin, bell pepper, tomato sauce, salt, pepper, ginger, coriander, turmeric, paprika, cayenne, garam masala and lemon juice.

Stir, cover and cook on high for 3 hours.

Stir your lentils mix again, divide into bowls and serve.

Enjoy!

Nutrition: calories 300, fat 6, fiber 5, carbs 9, protein 12

Delicious Butternut Squash Soup

Preparation time: 10 minutes

Cooking time: 6 hours

Servings: 8

Ingredients:

1 apple, cored, peeled and chopped

½ Pound carrots, chopped

1 pound butternut squash, peeled and cubed

1 yellow onion, chopped

A pinch of sea salt

Black pepper to the taste

1 bay leaf

3 cups veggie stock

14 ounces canned coconut milk

¼ Teaspoon sage, dried

Directions:

Put the stock in your slow cooker.

Add apple squash, carrots, onion, salt, pepper and bay leaf.

Stir, cover and cook on low for 6 hours.

Transfer to your blender, add coconut milk and sage and pulse really well.

Ladle into bowls and serve right away.

Enjoy!

Nutrition: calories 200, fat 3, fiber 6, carbs 8, protein 10

Amazing Mushroom Stew

Preparation time: 10 minutes

Cooking time: 8 hours

Servings: 4

Ingredients:

2 garlic cloves, minced

1 celery stalk, chopped

1 yellow onion, chopped

1 and ½ cups firm tofu, pressed and cubed

1 cup water

10 ounces mushrooms, chopped

1 pound mixed peas, corn and carrots

2 and ½ cups veggie stock

1 teaspoon thyme, dried

2 tablespoons coconut flour

A pinch of sea salt

Black pepper to the taste

Directions:

Put the water and stock in your slow cooker.

Add garlic, onion, celery, mushrooms, mixed veggies, tofu, thyme, salt, pepper and flour.

Stir everything, cover and cook on low for 8 hours.

Divide into bowls and serve hot.

Enjoy!

Nutrition: calories 230, fat 4, fiber 6, carbs 10, protein 7

Simple Tofu Dish

Preparation time: 10 minutes

Cooking time: 3 hours

Servings: 6

Ingredients:

1 big tofu package, cubed

1 tablespoon sesame oil

¼ Cup pineapple, cubed

1 tablespoon olive oil

2 garlic cloves, minced

1 tablespoons brown rice vinegar

2 teaspoon ginger, grated

¼ Cup soy sauce

5 big zucchinis, cubed

¼ Cup sesame seeds

Directions:

In your food processor, mix sesame oil with pineapple, olive oil, garlic, ginger, soy sauce and vinegar and whisk well.

Add this to your slow cooker and mix with tofu cubes.

Cover and cook on High for 2 hours and 45 minutes.

Add sesame seeds and zucchinis, stir gently, cover and cook on High for 15 minutes.

Divide between plates and serve.

Enjoy!

Nutrition: calories 200, fat 3, fiber 4, carbs 9, protein 10

Special Jambalaya

Preparation time: 10 minutes

Cooking time: 6 hours

Servings: 4

Ingredients:

6 ounces soy chorizo, chopped

1 and ½ cups celery ribs, chopped

1 cup okra

1 green bell pepper, chopped

16 ounces canned tomatoes and green chilies, chopped

2 garlic cloves, minced

½ Teaspoon paprika

1 and ½ cups veggie stock

A pinch of cayenne pepper

Black pepper to the taste

A pinch of salt

3 cups already cooked wild rice for serving

Directions:

Heat up a pan over medium high heat, add soy chorizo, stir, brown for a few minutes and transfer to your slow cooker.

Also, add celery, bell pepper, okra, tomatoes and chilies, garlic, paprika, salt, pepper and cayenne to your slow cooker.

Stir everything, add veggie stock, cover the slow cooker and cook on low for 6 hours.

Divide rice on plates, top each serving with your vegan jambalaya and serve hot.

Enjoy!

Nutrition: calories 150, fat 3, fiber 7, carbs 15, protein 9

Delicious Chard Soup

Preparation time: 10 minutes

Cooking time: 8 hours

Servings: 6

Ingredients:

1 yellow onion, chopped

1 tablespoon olive oil

1 celery stalk, chopped

2 garlic cloves, minced

1 carrot, chopped

1 bunch swiss chard, torn

1 cup brown lentils, dried

5 potatoes, peeled and cubed

1 tablespoon soy sauce

Black pepper to the taste

A pinch of sea salt

6 cups veggie stock

Directions:

Heat up a big pan with the oil over medium high heat, add onion, celery, garlic, carrot and Swiss chard, stir, cook for a few minutes and transfer to your slow cooker.

Also, add lentils, potatoes, soy sauce, salt, pepper and stock to the slow cooker, stir, cover and cook on Low for 8 hours.

Divide into bowls and serve hot.

Enjoy!

Nutrition: calories 200, fat 4, fiber 5, carbs 9, protein 12

Chinese Tofu and Veggies

Preparation time: 10 minutes

Cooking time: 4 hours

Servings: 4

Ingredients:

14 ounces extra firm tofu, pressed and cut into medium triangles

Cooking spray

2 teaspoons ginger, grated

1 yellow onion, chopped

3 garlic cloves, minced

8 ounces tomato sauce

¼ Cup hoisin sauce

¼ Teaspoon coconut aminos

2 tablespoons rice wine vinegar

1 tablespoon soy sauce

1 tablespoon spicy mustard

¼ Teaspoon red pepper, crushed

2 teaspoons molasses

2 tablespoons water

A pinch of black pepper

3 broccoli stalks

1 green bell pepper, cut into squares

2 zucchinis, cubed

Directions:

Heat up a pan over medium high heat, add tofu pieces, brown them for a few minutes and transfer to your slow cooker.

Heat up the pan again over medium high heat, add ginger, onion, garlic and tomato sauce, stir, sauté for a few minutes and transfer to your slow cooker as well.

Add hoisin sauce, aminos, vinegar, soy sauce, mustard, red pepper, molasses, water and black pepper, stir gently, cover and cook on high for 3 hours. Add zucchinis, bell pepper and broccoli, cover and cook on high for 1 more hour. Divide between plates and serve right away. Enjoy!

Nutrition: calories 300, fat 4, fiber 8, carbs 14, protein 13

Wonderful Corn Chowder

Preparation time: 10 minutes

Cooking time: 8 hours and 30 minutes

Servings: 6

Ingredients:

2 cups yellow onion, chopped

2 tablespoons olive oil

1 red bell pepper, chopped

1 pound gold potatoes, cubed

1 teaspoon cumin, ground

4 cups corn kernels

4 cups veggie stock

1 cup almond milk

A pinch of salt

A pinch of cayenne pepper

½ Teaspoon smoked paprika

Chopped scallions for serving

Directions:

Heat up a pan with the oil over medium heat, add onion, stir and sauté for 5 minutes and then transfer to your slow cooker.

Add bell pepper, 1 cup corn, potatoes, paprika, cumin, salt and cayenne, stir, cover and cook on low for 8 hours.

Blend this using an immersion blender and then mix with almond milk and the rest of the corn.

Stir chowder, cover and cook on low for 30 minutes more.

Ladle into bowls and serve with chopped scallions on top.

Enjoy!

Nutrition: calories 200, fat 4, fiber 7, carbs 13, protein 16

Black Eyed Peas Stew

Preparation time: 10 minutes

Cooking time: 4 hours

Servings: 8

Ingredients:

3 celery stalks, chopped

2 carrots, sliced

1 yellow onion, chopped

1 sweet potato, cubed

1 green bell pepper, chopped

3 cups black-eyed peas, soaked for 8 hours and drained

1 cup tomato puree

4 cups veggie stock

A pinch of salt

Black pepper to the taste

1 chipotle chile, minced

1 teaspoon ancho chili powder

1 teaspoons sage, dried and crumbled

2 teaspoons cumin, ground

Chopped coriander for serving

Directions:

Put celery in your slow cooker.

Add carrots, onion, potato, bell pepper, black-eyed peas, tomato puree, salt, pepper, chili powder, sage, chili, cumin and stock.

Stir, cover and cook on High for 4 hours.

Stir stew again, divide into bowls and serve with chopped coriander on top.

Enjoy!

Nutrition: calories 200, fat 4, fiber 7, carbs 9, protein 16

White Bean Cassoulet

Preparation time: 10 minutes

Cooking time: 6 hours

Servings: 4

Ingredients:

2 celery stalks, chopped

3 leeks, sliced

4 garlic cloves, minced

2 carrots, chopped

2 cups veggie stock

15 ounces canned tomatoes, chopped

1 bay leaf

1 tablespoon italian seasoning

30 ounces canned white beans, drained

For the breadcrumbs:

Zest from 1 lemon, grated

1 garlic clove, minced

2 tablespoons olive oil

1 cup vegan bread crumbs

¼ Cup parsley, chopped

Directions:

Heat up a pan with a splash of the veggie stock over medium heat, add celery and leeks, stir and cook for 2 minutes.

Add carrots and garlic, stir and cook for 1 minute more.

Add this to your slow cooker and mix with stock, tomatoes, bay leaf, italian seasoning and beans.

Stir, cover and cook on low for 6 hours.

Meanwhile, heat up a pan with the oil over medium high heat, add bread crumbs, lemon zest, 1 garlic clove and parsley, stir and toast for a couple of minutes.

Divide your white beans mix into bowls, sprinkle bread crumbs mix on top and serve.

Enjoy!

Nutrition: calories 223, fat 3, fiber 7, carbs 10, protein 7

Light Jackfruit Dish

Preparation time: 10 minutes

Cooking time: 6 hours

Servings: 4

Ingredients:

40 ounces green jackfruit in brine, drained

½ Cup agave nectar

½ Cup gluten free tamari sauce

¼ Cup soy sauce

1 cup white wine

2 tablespoons ginger, grated

8 garlic cloves, minced

1 pear, cored and chopped

1 yellow onion, chopped

½ Cup water

4 tablespoons sesame oil

Directions:

Put jackfruit in your slow cooker.

Add agave nectar, tamari sauce, soy sauce, wine, ginger, garlic, pear, onion, water and oil.

Stir well, cover and cook on low for 6 hours.

Divide jackfruit mix into bowls and serve.

Enjoy!

Nutrition: calories 160, fat 4, fiber 1, carbs 10, protein 3

Veggie Curry

Preparation time: 10 minutes

Cooking time: 4 hours

Servings: 4

Ingredients:

1 tablespoon ginger, grated

14 ounces canned coconut milk

Cooking spray

16 ounces firm tofu, pressed and cubed

1 cup veggie stock

¼ Cup green curry paste

½ Teaspoon turmeric

1 tablespoon coconut sugar

1 yellow onion, chopped

1 and ½ cup red bell pepper, chopped

A pinch of salt

¾ Cup peas

1 eggplant, chopped

Directions:

Put the coconut milk in your slow cooker.

Add ginger, stock, curry paste, turmeric, sugar, onion, bell pepper, salt, peas and eggplant pieces, stir, cover and cook on high for 4 hours.

Meanwhile, spray a pan with cooking spray and heat up over medium high heat.

Add tofu pieces and brown them for a few minutes on each side.

Divide tofu into bowls, add slowly cooked curry mix on top and serve.

Enjoy!

Nutrition: calories 200, fat 4, fiber 6, carbs 10, protein 9

Chapter 9. Burger And Sandwiches

Spicy Chickpea Sandwich

Preparation time: 10 minutes

Cooking time: 40 minutes

Servings: 4

Ingredients:

Raisins (.25 C.)

Spinach Leaves (.50 C.)

Red Onion (.50)

Red Pepper (.50)

Ground Cumin (.50 t.)

Turmeric (.25 t.)

Garam Masala Powder (1 T.)

Olive Oil (2 T.)

Garlic (1)

Chickpeas (14 Oz.)

Fresh Coriander (4 T.)

Salt (.25 t.)

Bread (8 Slices)

Directions:

To start, you will want to get out your blender. When you are set, add in the chickpeas, olive oil, juice of one lemon, and garlic clove. Blend everything together until the ingredients create a chunky paste.

With the chickpea paste made, transfer it into a bowl and mix in the cumin powder, turmeric, and the curry powder. Give everything a good stir to make sure there are no chunks in your chickpea paste.

Next, add in chopped onion and red pepper into the paste. At this point, you can also add in the chopped coriander and raisins. If you would like, feel free to season with salt and lemon juice at this point as well.

Finally, take your bread, spread the chickpea mix, top with some spinach leaves, and enjoy a nice protein packed sandwich!

Nutrition:

Calories: 280 Protein: 8g Fat: 8g

Carbs: 48g Fibers: 8g

Baked Spicy Tofu Sandwich

Preparation time: 10 minutes

Cooking time: 45 minutes

Servings: 4

Ingredients:

Whole Grain Bread (8)

Maple Syrup (1 T.)

White Miso Paste (1 T.)

Tomato Paste (1 T.)

Liquid Smoke (1 Dash)

Soy Sauce (1 T.)

Cumin (1 t.)

Paprika (.50 t.)

Chipotles in Adobo Sauce (1 t.)

Vegetable Broth (1 C.)

Tofu (16 Oz.)

Tomato (1)

Chopped Red Onion (.25 C.)

Tabasco (1 Dash)

Lime (1)

Cumin (.25 t.)

Chili Powder (.25 t.)

Coriander (.25 t.)

Cilantro (.25 C.)

Avocado (1)

Ground Black Pepper (.25 t.)

Garlic (2)

Lime (.50)

Directions:

To Prepare for this recipe, you will want to Preparation your tofu the night before. To start, you will want to press the tofu for a few hours. Once this is done, cut the tofu into eight slices and then place them in the freezer.

When you are ready, it is time to make the marinade for the tofu. To do this, take a bowl and mix together the vegetable broth, tomato paste, maple syrup, and all of the spices from the list above. Be sure to stir everything together to get the spices spread through the vegetable broth. Once it is mixed together, add in your thawed slices of tofu and soak them for a few hours.

Once the tofu is marinated, heat your oven to 425 degrees. When the oven is warm, place the tofu on a baking sheet and place in the oven for twenty minutes. At the end of this time, the tofu should be nice and crispy on the top and edges.

When your tofu is cooked to your liking, layer it on your bread slices with your favorite toppings. This sandwich can be enjoyed cold or warm!

Nutrition:

Calories: 390

Protein: 21g

Fat: 16g

Carbs: 49g

Fibers: 11g

Lentil Burgers

Preparation time: 10 minutes

Cooking time: 15 minutes

Servings: 4

Ingredients:

Bread Crumbs (2 T.)

Crushed Walnuts (2 T.)

Soy Sauce (1 t.)

Cooked Lentils (2 C.)

Salt (.50 t.)

Cumin (.25 t.)

Nutritional Yeast (.25 C.)

Directions:

First, you will want to cook your two cups of lentils. You will want to complete this task following the Preparation provided on the side of the package. Once this step is complete, drain the lentils and place them into a medium-sized bowl. When the lentils are in place, gently mash them until they reach a smooth consistency.

At this point, you will want to add in the bread crumbs, crushed walnuts, soy sauce, nutritional yeast, cumin, and the salt. Be sure to mix everything together and then begin to form your patties. They should be about four inches in diameter and only an inch thick.

With your patties formed, you will want to heat a medium size pan over medium heat and begin to warm it. Once warm, add in oil and cook each patty for two to three minutes on each side. By the end, each side of the burger should be crisp and brown.

Finally, serve on a warm bun with your favorite vegan condiments and garnish!

Nutrition: Calories: 410, Protein: 31g, Fat: 5g, Carbs: 65g, Fibers: 33g

Sweet Hawaiian Burger

Preparation time: 10 minutes

Cooking time: 15 minutes

Servings: 4

Ingredients:

Panko Breadcrumbs (1 C.)

Red Kidney Beans (14 Oz.)

Vegetable Oil (1 T.)

Diced Sweet Potato (1.50 C.)

Minced Garlic (1)

Soy Sauce (2 T.)

Apple Cider Vinegar (3 T.)

Maple Syrup (.50 C.)

Water (.50 C.)

Tomato Paste (.50 C.)

Pineapple Rings (4)

Salt (.25 t.)

Pepper (.25 t.)

Cayenne (.10 t.)

Ground Cumin (1.50 t.)

Burger Buns (4)

Optional: Red Onion, Tomato, Lettuce, Vegan Mayo

Directions:

First, you will want to heat your oven to 400 degrees. As the oven warms up, take your sweet potato and toss it in oil. When this step is complete, place the diced sweet potato pieces in a single layer on a baking sheet. Once this is done, pop the sheet into the oven and cook for about twenty minutes. Halfway through, flip the pieces over to assure the sweet potato cooks all the way through. When this is done, remove the sheet from the oven and allow the sweet potato to cool down slightly.

Next, you will want to get out your food processor. When you are ready, add in the beans, sweet potatoes, breadcrumbs, cayenne, cumin, soy sauce, garlic, and onion pieces. Once in place, begin to pulse the ingredients together until you have a finely chopped mixture. As you do this, season the "dough" with pepper and salt as desired. Now, shape the dough into four patties.

When your patties are formed, begin to heat a large skillet over medium heat. As the pan warms up, place your oil and then grill each side of your patties. Typically, this will take five to six minutes on each side. You will know the burger is cooked through when it is browned on each side.

All you need to do now is assemble your burger! If you want, try baking the pineapple rings—three minutes on each side should do the trick! Top your burger with lettuce, tomato, and vegan mayo for some extra flavor.

Nutrition:

Calories: 460

Protein: 15g

Fat: 12g

Carbs: 80g

Fibers: 6g

Tofu & Veggie Burgers

Preparation time: 20 minutes

Cooking time: 8 minutes

Servings: 2

Ingredients

Patties

½ cup firm tofu, pressed and drained

1 medium carrot, peeled and grated

1 tablespoon onion, chopped

1 tablespoon scallion, chopped

1 tablespoon fresh parsley, chopped

½ garlic clove, minced

2 teaspoons low-sodium soy sauce

1 tablespoon cornflour

1 teaspoon nutritional yeast flakes

½ teaspoon Dijon mustard

1 teaspoon paprika

¼ teaspoon ground turmeric

½ teaspoon ground black pepper

2 tablespoons canola oil

For Serving

1 small avocado, peeled, pitted, and sliced

½ cup cherry tomatoes, halved

2 cup fresh baby greens

How to Prepare

For patties: in a bowl, add the tofu and with a fork, mash well.

Add the remaining ingredients (except for oil) and mix until well combined.

Make 4 equal-sized patties from the mixture.

Heat the oil in a frying pan over low heat and cook the patties for about 4 minutes per side.

Divide the avocado, tomatoes, and greens onto serving plates.

Top each plate with 2 patties and serve.

Nutrition

Calories 342   Total Fat 28.5 g   Saturated Fat 4 g

Cholesterol 0 mg   Sodium 335 mg   Total Carbs 17.7 g

Fiber 7.7 g Sugar 4.5 g   Protein 10 g

Buckwheat Burgers

Preparation time: 20 minutes

Cooking time: 45 minutes

Total time: 1 hour 5 minutes

Servings: 2

Ingredients

Patties

¾ cup dry buckwheat

1½ cups water

Salt, to taste

2 tablespoons olive oil, divided

½ of large yellow onion, chopped finely

½ of large carrot, peeled and grated

½ celery stalk, chopped finely

1 fresh kale leaf, tough ribs removed and chopped finely

1 large cooked sweet potato, mashed

2 tablespoons almond butter

2 tablespoons low-sodium soy sauce

For Serving

3 cups fresh baby greens

1 cup cherry tomatoes, halved

1 cup purple cabbage, shredded

1 yellow bell pepper, seeded and sliced

How to Prepare

Preheat oven to 350ºF and line a baking sheet with parchment paper.

For patties: heat a non-stick frying pan over medium heat and toast the buckwheat for about 5 minutes, stirring continuously.

Add the water and salt and bring to a boil over high heat.

Reduce the heat to low and cook, covered for about 15 minutes or until all the water is absorbed.

Meanwhile, heat 1 tablespoon of the oil in a skillet over medium heat and sauté the onion for about 4–5 minutes.

Add the carrot and celery and cook for about 5 minutes.

Stir in the remaining ingredients and remove from the heat.

Transfer the mixture into a bowl with buckwheat and stir to combine.

Set aside to cool completely.

Make 4 equal-sized patties from the mixture.

Arrange the patties onto the Prepared baking sheet in a single layer and bake for about 20 minutes per side.

Divide the greens, tomatoes, cabbage, and bell pepper onto serving plates.

Top each plate with 2 patties and serve

Nutrition

Calories 588   Total Fat 25.2 g   Saturated Fat 3.1 g

Cholesterol 0 mg   Sodium 1000 mg   Total Carbs 84.8 g

Fiber 15.4 g   Sugar 16.4 g   Protein 16.7 g

Chapter 10.   Dinner Recipes

Green Curry Tofu

Preparation time: 10 minutes

Cooking time: 15 minutes

Servings: 1

Ingredients:

Lime Juice (1 T.)

Tamari Sauce (1 T.)

Water Chestnuts (8 Oz.)

Green Beans (1 C.)

Salt (.50 t.)

Vegetable Broth (.50 C.)

Coconut Milk (14 Oz.)

Chickpeas (1 C.)

Green Curry Paste (3 T.)

Frozen Edamame (1 C.)

Garlic Cloves (2)

Ginger (1 inch)

Olive Oil (1 t.)

Diced Onion (1)

Extra-firm Tofu (8 Oz.)

Brown Basmati Rice (1 C.)

Directions:

To start, you will want to cook your rice according to the Preparation on the package. You can do this in a rice cooker or simply on top of the stove.

Next, you will want to Prepare your tofu. You can remove the tofu from the package and set it on a plate. Once in place, set another plate on top and something heavy so you can begin to drain the tofu. Once the tofu is Prepared, cut it into half inch cubes.

Next, take a medium-sized pan and place it over medium heat. As the pan heats up, go ahead and place your olive oil. When the olive oil begins to sizzle, add your onions and cook until they turn a nice translucent color. Typically, this process will take about five minutes. When your onions are ready, add in the garlic and ginger. With these in place, cook the ingredients for another two to three minutes.

Once the last step is done, add in your curry paste and edamame. Cook these two ingredients until the edamame is no longer frozen.

With these ready, you will now add in the cubed tofu, chickpeas, vegetable broth, coconut milk, and the salt. When everything is in place, you will want to bring the pot to a simmer. Add in the water chestnuts and green beans next and cook for a total of five minutes.

When all of the ingredients are cooked through, you can remove the pan from the heat and divide your meal into bowls. For extra flavor, try stirring in tamari, lime juice, or soy sauce. This recipe is excellent served over rice or any other side dish!

Nutrition: Calories: 760, Protein: 23g, Fat: 38g

Carbs: 89g, Fibers: 9g

African Peanut Protein Stew

Preparation time: 10 minutes

Cooking time: 30 minutes

Servings: 4

Ingredients:

Basmati Rice (1 Package)

Roasted Peanuts (.25 C.)

Baby Spinach (2 C.)

Chickpeas (15 Oz.)

Chili Powder (1.50 t.)

Vegetable Broth (4 C.)

Natural Peanut Butter (.33 C.)

Pepper (.25 t.)

Salt (.25 t.)

Diced Tomatoes (28 Oz.)

Chopped Sweet Potato (1)

Diced Jalapeno (1)

Diced Red Pepper (1)

Sweet Onion (1)

Olive Oil (1 t.)

Directions:

First, you will want to cook your onion. You will do this by heating olive oil in a large saucepan over medium heat. Once the olive oil is sizzling, add in the onion and cook for five minutes or so. The onion will turn translucent when it is cooked through.

With the onion done, you will now add in the canned tomatoes, diced sweet potato, jalapeno, and bell peppers. Simmer all of these ingredients over a medium to high heat for about five minutes. If desired, you can season these vegetables with salt and pepper.

As the vegetables cook, you will want to make your sauce. You will do this by taking a bowl and mix together one cup of vegetable broth with the peanut butter. Be sure to mix well, so there are no clumps. Once this is done, pour the sauce into the saucepan along with three more cups of vegetable broth. At this point, you will want to season the dish with cayenne and chili powder.

Next, cover your pan and reduce to a lower heat. Go ahead and allow these ingredients to simmer for about ten to twenty minutes. At the end of this time, the sweet potato should be nice and tender.

Last, you will want to add in the spinach and chickpeas. Give everything a good stir to mix together. You will want to cook this dish until the spinach begins to wilt. Once again, you can add salt and pepper as needed.

Finally, serve your dish over rice, garnish with peanuts, and enjoy!

Nutrition:

Calories: 440

Protein: 16g

Fat: 13g

Carbs: 69g

Fibers: 12g

Thai Zucchini Noodle Salad

Preparation time: 10 minutes

Cooking time: 35 minutes

Servings: 4

Ingredients:

Peanuts (.50 C.)

Peanut Sauce (.50 C.), Water (2 T.)

Extra-firm Tofu (.50 Block)

Chopped Green Onions (.25 C.)

Spiralized Carrot (1), Spiralized Zucchini (3)

Directions: First, you are going to want to create your peanut sauce. To do this, take a small bowl and slowly mix your peanut sauce with water. You will want to add one tablespoon at a time to achieve the thickness you desire. Next, you will combine all of the ingredients from above, minus the peanuts, into a large mixing bowl. Once everything is in place, top with the salad dressing and give everything a good toss to assure even coating. Finally, sprinkle your peanuts on top, and your meal is done!

Nutrition: Calories: 200, Protein: 13g, Fat: 13g, Carbs: 11g, Fibers: 5g

Split Pea and Cauliflower Stew

Preparation time: 10 minutes

Cooking time: 60 minutes

Servings: 4

Ingredients:

Green Onions (.25 C.)

Chopped Cilantro (.25 C.)

Salt (1.50 t.)

Garam Masala (1 t.)

Apple Cider Vinegar (2 t.)

Light Coconut Milk (15 Oz.)

Vegetable Broth (2 C.)

Ground Turmeric (1 t.)

Curry Powder (3 t.)

Minced Garlic (6)

Chopped Carrots (2)

Chopped Onion (1)

Cumin Seeds (1 t.)

Mustard Seeds (1 t.)

Spinach Leaves (3 C.)

Chopped Cauliflower (1)

Cooked Split Peas (2 C.)

Directions:

Before you begin cooking this recipe, you will want to Prepare your split peas according to the Preparation on their package.

Once your split peas are cooked, you will want to preheat your oven to 375 degrees. Once warm, place your chopped cauliflower pieces onto a baking sheet and pop it into the oven for ten to fifteen minutes. By the end, the cauliflower should be tender and slightly brown.

Next, you will want to place a large pot on your stove and turn the heat to medium. As the pot heats up, add in the oil, cumin seeds, and mustard seeds. Within sixty seconds, the seeds will begin popping. You will want to make sure you are stirring these ingredients frequently, so they do not burn.

Now that the seeds and oil are warm, you can add in your onion, garlic, ginger, and chopped carrots. Cook these for five minutes or until the carrot and onion are nice and soft. Once they are, you can add in your turmeric and curry powder. Be sure to gently mix everything together so you can evenly coat the vegetables.

After one minute of allowing the vegetables to soak up the spices, you will want to add in the coconut milk, split peas, and vegetable broth. At this point, you will want to lower the heat to low and place a cover over your pot. Allow all of the ingredients to simmer for about twenty minutes. As everything cooks, be sure to stir the pot occasionally to make sure nothing sticks to the bottom.

Finally, you will want to stir in the garam masala, apple cider vinegar, and the roasted cauliflower. If needed, you can also add salt as desired. When these ingredients are in place, go ahead and allow the stew to simmer for another ten minutes or so.

As a final touch, feel free to top your stew with green onions and chopped cilantro for extra flavors!

Nutrition: Calories: 700, Protein: 31g, Fat: 31g, Carbs: 84g, Fibers: 34g

Black Bean and Pumpkin Chili

Preparation time: 10 minutes

Cooking time: 15 minutes

Servings: 4

Ingredients:

Garbanzo Beans (1 Can)

Black Beans (1 Can)

Vegetable Stock (1 C.)

Tomatoes (1 C.)

Pumpkin Puree (1 C.)

Chopped Onion (1)

Olive Oil (1 T.)

Chili Powder (2 T.)

Cumin Powder (1 T.)

Salt (.25 t.)

Pepper (.25 t.)

Directions:

To begin, you will want to place a large pot over medium heat. At the pot warms up, place your olive oil, garlic, and chopped onion into the bottom. Allow this mixture to cook for about five minutes or until the onion is soft.

At this point, you will now want to add in the garbanzo beans, black beans, vegetable stock, canned tomatoes, and pumpkin. If you do not have any vegetable stock on hand, you can also use water.

With your ingredients in place, add in the half of the chili powder, half of the cumin, and any salt and pepper according to your own taste. Once the spices are in place, give the chili a quick taste and add more as needed.

Now, bring the pot to a boil and stir all of the ingredients together to assure the spices are spread evenly throughout your dish.

Last, bring the pot to a simmer and cook everything for about twenty minutes. When the twenty minutes are done, remove the pot from the heat, and enjoy!

Nutrition: Calories: 390, Protein: 19g, Fat: 8g, Carbs: 65g, Fibers: 21g

Matcha Tofu Soup

Preparation time: 10 minutes

Cooking time: 55 minutes

Servings: 4

Ingredients:

Vegetable Broth (.5 0 C.)

Extra-firm Tofu (1 Package)

Light Coconut Milk (13.5 Oz.)

Kale (5 C.)

Garlic Powder (.25 t.)

Smoked Paprika (.25 t)

Ground Black Pepper (.25 t.)

Mirin (1 t.)

Soy Sauce (2 T.)

Cilantro (1 C.)

Matcha Powder (2 t.)

Vegetable Broth (4 C.)

Ground Black Pepper (.25 t.)

Cayenne Pepper (.25 t.)

Garlic (1 t.)

Minced Garlic (3)

Chopped Potato (1)

Chopped Onion (1)

Directions:

To start, you will want to place a large pot over medium heat. As the pot warms up, add a splash of vegetable broth to the bottom and begin to cook the chopped potato and onion. Typically, it will take eight to ten minutes until they are nice and soft. When the vegetables are ready, you can then add in the black pepper, cayenne pepper, ginger, and garlic. Sauté these ingredients for another minute.

When these vegetables are Prepared, you can add in the kale and cook for a few more minutes. Once the kale begins to wilt, stir in the rest of the vegetable broth and bring your soup to a boil. Once boiling, reduce the heat, cover the pot, and simmer all of the ingredients for thirty minutes. After fifteen minutes, remove the top so you can stir in the matcha and cilantro.

Once the thirty minutes are done, remove the pot from the heat and allow the soup to cool for a little. Once cool, place the mixture into a blender and gently stir in the coconut milk. Blend the soup on high until you reach a silky and smooth consistency for the soup.

Finally, cook your tofu according to your own preference. Be sure to chop the tofu into cubes and brown on all sides. Once cooked, place the tofu in your soup and enjoy!

Nutrition: Calories: 450, Protein: 20g, Fat: 32g, Carbs: 27g, Fibers: 7g

Sweet Potato Tomato Soup

Preparation time: 10 minutes

Cooking time: 15 minutes

Servings: 4

Ingredients:

Water or Vegetable Stock (1 L.)

Tomato Puree (2 T.)

Garlic (3)

Chopped Onion (1)

Red Lentils (1 C.)

Chopped Carrots (3)

Chopped Sweet Potato (1)

Salt (.25 t.)

Pepper (.25 t.)

Ginger (.50 t.)

Chili Powder (.50 t.)

Directions:

First, we are going to prepare the vegetables for this recipe. You will do this by preheating your oven to 350 degrees. While the oven heats up, you will want to peel and cut both your sweet potato and the carrots. Once they are prepared, place them on a baking sheet and drizzle them with olive oil. You can also add salt and pepper if you would like. When you are ready, place the sheet into the oven for forty minutes. By the end, the vegetables should be nice and soft.

As the sweet potato and carrots get baked in the oven, place a medium-sized pan over medium heat and begin to cook your garlic and onion. After five minutes or so, you will want to add in your cooked lentils, tomato, and the spices from the list above. By the end, the lentils should be soft.

Finally, you will add all of the ingredients into a blender and blend until the soup if perfectly smooth.

Nutrition:

Calories: 350   Protein: 16g

Fat: 11g   Carbs: 48g   Fibers: 19g

Baked Spicy Tofu Sandwich

Preparation time: 10 minutes

Cooking time: 45 minutes

Servings: 4

Ingredients:

Whole Grain Bread (8)

Maple Syrup (1 T.)

White Miso Paste (1 T.)

Tomato Paste (1 T.)

Liquid Smoke (1 Dash)

Soy Sauce (1 T.)

Cumin (1 t.)

Paprika (.50 t.)

Chipotles in Adobo Sauce (1 t.)

Vegetable Broth (1 C.)

Tofu (16 Oz.)

Tomato (1)

Chopped Red Onion (.25 C.)

Tabasco (1 Dash)

Lime (1)

Cumin (.25 t.)

Chili Powder (.25 t.)

Coriander (.25 t.)

Cilantro (.25 C.)

Avocado (1)

Ground Black Pepper (.25 t.)

Garlic (2)

Lime (.50)

Directions:

To prepare for this recipe, you will want to prep your tofu the night before. To start, you will want to press the tofu for a few hours. Once this is done, cut the tofu into eight slices and then place them in the freezer.

When you are ready, it is time to make the marinade for the tofu. To do this, take a bowl and mix together the vegetable broth, tomato paste, maple syrup, and all of the spices from the list above. Be sure to stir everything together to get the spices spread through the vegetable broth. Once it is mixed together, add in your thawed slices of tofu and soak them for a few hours.

Once the tofu is marinated, heat your oven to 425 degrees. When the oven is warm, place the tofu on a baking sheet and place in the oven for twenty minutes. At the end of this time, the tofu should be nice and crispy on the top and edges.

When your tofu is cooked to your liking, layer it on your bread slices with your favorite toppings. This sandwich can be enjoyed cold or warm!

Nutrition:

Calories: 390

Protein: 21g

Fat: 16g

Carbs: 49g

Fibers: 11g

Vegetable Stir-Fry

Preparation time: 10 minutes

Cooking time: 45 minutes

Servings: Three

Ingredients:

Zucchini (.50)

Red Bell Pepper (.50)

Broccoli (.50)

Red Cabbage (1 C.)

Brown Rice (.50 C.)

Tamari Sauce (2 T.)

Red Chili Pepper (1)

Fresh Parsley (.25 t.)

Garlic (4)

Olive Oil (2 T.)

Optional: Sesame Seeds

Directions:

To begin, you will want to cook your brown rice according to the directions that are placed on the package. Once this step is done, place the brown rice in a bowl and put it to the side.

Next, you will want to take a frying pan and place some water in the bottom. Bring the pan over medium heat and then add in your chopped vegetables. Once in place, cook the vegetables for five minutes or until they are tender.

When the vegetables are cooked through, you will then want to add in the parsley, cayenne powder, and the garlic. You will want to cook this mixture for a minute or so. Be sure you stir the ingredients so that nothing sticks to the bottom of your pan.

Now, add in the rice and tamari to your pan. You will cook this mixture for a few more minutes or until everything is warmed through.

For extra flavor, try adding sesame seeds before you enjoy your lunch! If you have any leftovers, you can keep this stir-fry in a sealed container for about five days in your fridge.

Nutrition:

Calories: 280   Protein: 10g

Fat: 12g   Carbs: 38g   Fibers: 6g

Creamy Tomato Lentil Soup

Preparation Time: 10 minutes

Cooking Time: 35 minutes

Servings: 4

Ingredients:

1 medium yellow onion, chopped

2 bay leaves

½ tsp. sea salt

½ tsp. black pepper

3 medium tomato, chopped

1/3 cup coconut milk

1/3 cup tomato paste

1 cup mixed lentils

1 cup vegetable broth

1 tsp. paprika

3 tbsp. olive oil

Method:

Heat oil in a medium-sized pot, and once hot, add the onion to it. Cook them for 5 minutes or until softened. Stir in the lentils, paprika and bay leaves to the pot and cook for 2 minutes or until fragrant. Add tomato paste, vegetable stock and chopped tomato to it. Bring the stock mixture to boiling and allow it to cook for 15 to 20 minutes. Tip: add water if it seems dry. Taste to season, and add more salt and pepper as needed.

Before serving, swirl the coconut milk over it. Serve it hot. Tip: You can also blend in a high-speed blender for a smoother soup.

Nutritional Information Per Serving: Calories: 346Kcal

Protein: 15g Carbohydrates: 42g Fat: 15g

Chili Carne

Preparation Time: 10 minutes

Cooking Time: 40 minutes

Servings: 6

Ingredients:

2 celery stalks, chopped finely

Salt and pepper, to taste

2 tbsp. oil

1 tsp. chili powder

2 carrots, chopped

3 ½ oz. split red lentils

3 garlic cloves, minced

14 oz. soy mince

1 large red onion, sliced thinly

14 oz. red kidney beans, drained and washed

1 tsp. cumin, ground

2 red peppers, chopped finely

1 ¾ lb. chopped tomatoes

1 cup vegetable stock

Method:

Heat oil in a large-sized skillet.

When the oil is hot, stir in the onion, peppers, garlic, carrot and celery, and sauté them for 3 minutes or until softened.

Spoon in cumin, chili powder, pepper and salt. Mix.

Add chopped tomatoes, soy mince, vegetable stock, kidney beans and lentils. Combine well.

Bring the mixture to a simmer.

Taste for seasoning and add more salt and pepper as needed.

Serve hot.

Tip: Pair it with basmati rice and a squeeze of lime juice.

Nutritional Information Per Serving: Calories: 340Kcal

Protein: 25g Carbohydrates: 42g Fat: 8g

Mexican Lentil Stew

Preparation Time: 10 minutes

Cooking Time: 45 minutes

Servings: 6

Ingredients:

½ tsp. salt

1 yellow onion, diced

8 cups vegetable broth

1 avocado, diced

2 carrots, peeled and diced

2 cups lentils, (preferably green) washed

1 red bell pepper, diced

2 tbsp. extra virgin olive oil

1 tbsp. cumin

2 celery stalks, diced

Cilantro, as needed, for garnishing

3 garlic cloves, minced

¼ tsp. smoked paprika

2 × 4 oz. diced green chili

1 tsp. oregano

2 cups diced tomatoes

Method:

You need to heat oil in a large pot over medium heat.

When the oil is hot, stir in the bell pepper, onion, celery and carrot.

Sauté them for 4 to 5 minutes or until softened.

Next, spoon in garlic, oregano, cumin and paprika. Mix and cook for a minute.

Stir in lentils, tomatoes, chili, broth and salt to it. Bring the mixture to a boil.

Simmer the stew for 30 to 40 minutes or until the lentils are tender. Keep the lid tilted.

Taste for seasoning and add more salt and pepper as needed.

Serve it hot.

Tip: Top with coriander and avocado slices.

Nutritional Information Per Serving:

Calories: 429Kcal

Protein: 25.1g

Carbohydrates: 51.9g

Fat: 14.2g

Lentil Meatloaf

Preparation Time: 10 minutes

Cooking Time: 45 minutes

Servings: 4 to 6

Ingredients:

1 cup green lentils

½ tsp. salt

2 cups water

1 tsp. basil, dried

¼ tsp. pepper

1 tsp. olive oil

1 tsp. garlic powder

2 tbsp. flaxseeds

4 tbsp. water

1 cup tomato sauce

1 yellow onion, diced

1 cup regular steel cut oats

1 tsp. parsley, dried

¼ cup BBQ sauce

2 tbsp. ketchup

Method:

Boil water in a pot over medium-high heat.

Once boiling, add the lentils and cook them for 30 minutes or until cooked. Drain the water and mash the lentils slightly. Transfer to a bowl and allow to cool.Combine the flaxseed with the water in another bowl and set it aside for 15 minutes. Heat oil in a medium-sized skillet over medium heat.

Stir in the onion and cook for 4 to 5 minutes or until softened. Next, add the onion and oats to the lentils along with the remaining ingredients, apart from the BBQ sauce and ketchup. Stir well until everything comes together. Transfer the dough to a well-greased loaf pan and smooth out the top. Spoon the ketchup and BBQ sauce over it. Bake for 43 to 45 minutes at 350°F or until it is golden brown and firm. Tip: Top with additional BBQ sauce if desired.

Nutritional Information Per Serving: Calories: 987Kcal

Protein: 34g Carbohydrates: 165g Fat: 26g

Black Bean Soup

Preparation Time: 10 minutes

Cooking Time: 25 minutes

Servings: 6

Ingredients:

4 cups black beans, cooked

1 medium onion, diced

14 ½ oz. diced tomatoes

2 garlic cloves, minced

4 cups vegetable broth

1 tsp. cumin

1 red bell pepper, diced

½ tsp. oregano, dried

½ tsp. salt

½ tsp. smoked paprika

Method:

Begin by heating a pot over a medium-high heat.

When hot, stir in the onion, red bell pepper and garlic along with ¼ cup of water.

Cook for 6 minutes or until the veggies have softened

Stir in the seasoning and cook for another 2 minutes

Add beans, vegetable broth and tomato BBQ to it. Combine.

Bring the broth mixture to a boil and lower the heat to sim.

Allow it to simmer for 20 minutes.

Finally, pour the soup into a high-speed blender.

Tip: Top with additional BBQ sauce.

Nutritional Information Per Serving:

Calories: 987Kcal

Protein: 34g

Carbohydrates: 165g

Mushroom Pasta

Preparation Time: 10 minutes

Cooking Time: 30 minutes

Servings: 6

Ingredients:

2 green onions, sliced thinly

12 oz. mixed mushrooms, sliced thinly

1 lb. linguine

3 garlic cloves, chopped finely

½ tsp. salt

¼ cup nutritional yeast

6 tbsp. oil

¾ tsp. black pepper, ground

Method:

Cook the linguine by following the instructions on the packet.

Once the pasta is cooked, reserve ¾ cup of the pasta water. Drain the remaining water and transfer the cooked pasta into a pot.

Spoon oil into a large saucepan and heat it over medium-high heat.

Stir in the mushrooms and garlic.

Sauté for 4 minutes or until the mushrooms become tender. Stir frequently.

Combine the mushrooms with the linguine, nutritional yeast, salt, pepper and ¾ cup of the water. Mix until everything comes together.

Garnish it with green onions. Tip: You could try adding bell peppers to the dish.

Nutritional Information Per Serving: Calories: 430Kcal

Protein: 15g Carbohydrates: 62g Fat: 15g

Lemon Pasta Alfredo

Preparation Time: 10 minutes

Cooking Time: 35 minutes

Servings: 4

Ingredients:

3 tbsp. almonds, blanched & sliced

12 oz. eggless pasta

1 tsp. lemon zest, finely grated

2 cups almond milk, unsweetened

2 tbsp. extra virgin olive oil

4 oz. soy cream cheese

3 garlic cloves, minced

Salt and black Pepper, as needed

3 tbsp. nutritional yeast plus for garnishing

½ cup fresh parsley, chopped

Method:

Cook the pasta in a pot of boiling water over a medium-high heat by following the instructions given in the packet. Drain the water, keeping 1 cup of the pasta water aside.

Put the nutritional yeast, ¼ teaspoon pepper, almond milk, one teaspoon salt, soy cream cheese, almonds into a blender.

Blend for 2 minutes or until smooth.

Spoon in oil and garlic to a large skillet and heat it over a medium-high heat.

Cook for one minute or until the garlic is aromatic.

Stir in the almond milk mixture along with ½ cup of the reserved pasta water.

Bring the mixture to a gentle boil and allow it to simmer for 6 to 8 minutes or until thick and creamy. Remove the skillet from the stove and add the pasta. Mix well. Tip: If it seems too thickened, add a bit of water. Transfer the mixture to the serving bowls and garnish with parsley and nutritional yeast. Tip: Instead of almonds, you can also use walnuts.

Nutritional Information Per Serving: Calories: 520Kcal

Protein: 22g Carbohydrates: 74g Fat: 15g

Chapter 11. Dessert And Snacks

Banana-Nut Bread Bars

Preparation time: 5 minutes

Cooking time: 30 minutes

Servings: 9 bars

Ingredients

Nonstick cooking spray (optional)

2 large ripe bananas

1 tablespoon maple syrup

½ Teaspoon vanilla extract

2 cups old-fashioned rolled oats

½ Teaspoons salt

¼ Cup chopped walnuts

Directions:

Preheat the oven to 350°f. Lightly coat a 9-by-9-inch baking pan with nonstick cooking spray (if using) or line with parchment paper for oil-free baking.

In a medium bowl, mash the bananas with a fork. Add the maple syrup and vanilla extract and mix well. Add the oats, salt, and walnuts, mixing well.

Transfer the batter to the baking pan and bake for 25 to 30 minutes, until the top is crispy. Cool completely before slicing into 9 bars. Transfer to an airtight storage container or a large plastic bag.

Nutrition (1 bar): calories: 73; fat: 1g; protein: 2g; carbohydrates: 15g; fiber: 2g; sugar: 5g; sodium: 129mg

Lemon Coconut Cilantro Rolls

Preparation time: 30 minutes chill time: 30 minutes

Servings: 16 pieces

Ingredients

½ Cup fresh cilantro, chopped

1 cup sprouts (clover, alfalfa)

1 garlic clove, pressed

2 tablespoons ground brazil nuts or almonds

2 tablespoons flaked coconut

1 tablespoon coconut oil

Pinch cayenne pepper

Pinch sea salt

Pinch freshly ground black pepper

Zest and juice of 1 lemon

2 tablespoons ground flaxseed

1 to 2 tablespoons water

2 whole-wheat wraps, or corn wraps

Directions:

Put everything but the wraps in a food processor and pulse to combine. Or combine the Ingredients in a large bowl. Add the water, if needed, to help the mix come together.

Spread the mixture out over each wrap, roll it up, and place it in the fridge for 30 minutes to set.

Remove the rolls from the fridge and slice each into 8 pieces to serve as appetizers or sides with a soup or stew.

Get the best flavor by buying whole raw brazil nuts or almonds, toasting them lightly in a dry skillet or toaster oven, and then grinding them in a coffee grinder.

Nutrition (1 piece) calories: 66; total fat: 4g; carbs: 6g; fiber: 1g; protein: 2g

Tamari Almonds

Preparation time: 5 minutes

Cooking time: 15 minutes

Servings: 8

Ingredients

1 pound raw almonds

3 tablespoons tamari or soy sauce

2 tablespoons extra-virgin olive oil

1 tablespoon Nutritional yeast

1 to 2 teaspoons chili powder, to taste

Directions: Preheat the oven to 400°f. Line a baking sheet with parchment paper. In a medium bowl, combine the almonds, tamari, and olive oil until well coated. Spread the almonds on the Prepared baking sheet and roast for 10 to 15 minutes, until browned. Cool for 10 minutes, then season with the Nutritional yeast and chili powder. Transfer to a glass jar and close tightly with a lid.

Nutrition: calories: 364; fat: 32g; protein: 13g; carbohydrates: 13g; fiber: 7g; sugar: 3g; sodium: 381mg

Tempeh Taco Bites

Preparation time: 5 minutes

Cooking time: 45 minutes

Servings: 3 dozen

Ingredients

8 ounces tempeh

3 tablespoons soy sauce

2 teaspoons ground cumin

1 teaspoon chili powder

1 teaspoon dried oregano

1 tablespoon olive oil

1/2 cup finely minced onion

2 garlic cloves, minced

Salt and freshly ground black pepper

2 tablespoons tomato paste

1 chipotle chile in adobo, finely minced

1/4 cup hot water or vegetable broth, homemade or store-bought, plus more if needed

36 phyllo pastry cups, thawed

1/2 cup basic guacamole, homemade or store-bought

18 ripe cherry tomatoes, halved

Preparation

In a medium saucepan of simmering water, cook the tempeh for 30 minutes. Drain well, then finely mince and place it in a bowl. Add the soy sauce, cumin, chili powder, and oregano. Mix well and set aside.

In a medium skillet, heat the oil over medium heat. Add the onion, cover, and cook for 5 minutes. Stir in the garlic, then add the tempeh mixture and cook, stirring, for 2 to 3 minutes. Season with salt and pepper to taste. Set aside. In a small bowl, combine the tomato paste, chipotle, and the hot water or broth. Return tempeh mixture to heat and in stir tomato-chile mixture and cook for 10 to 15 minutes, stirring occasionally, until the liquid is absorbed. The mixture should be fairly dry, but if it begins to stick to the pan, add a little more hot water, 1 tablespoon at a time. Taste, adjusting seasonings if necessary. Remove from the heat. To assemble, fill the phyllo cups to the top with the tempeh filling, using about 2 teaspoons of filling in each. Top with a dollop of guacamole and a cherry tomato half and serve.

Mushroom Croustades

Preparation time: 10 minutes

Cooking time: 10 minutes

Servings: 12 croustades

Ingredients

12 thin slices whole-grain bread

1 tablespoon olive oil, plus more for brushing bread

2 medium shallots, chopped

2 garlic cloves, minced

12 ounces white mushrooms, chopped

1/4 cup chopped fresh parsley

1 teaspoon dried thyme

1 tablespoon soy sauce

Preparation

Preheat the oven to 400°f. Using a 3-inch round pastry cutter or a drinking glass, cut a circle from each bread slice. Brush the bread circles with oil and press them firmly but gently into a mini-muffin tin. Bake until the bread is toasted, about 10 minutes.

Meanwhile, in a large skillet, heat the 1 tablespoon oil over medium heat. Add the shallots, garlic, and mushrooms and sauté for 5 minutes to soften the vegetables. Stir in the parsley, thyme, and soy sauce and cook until the liquid is absorbed, about 5 minutes longer. Spoon the mushroom mixture into the croustade cups and return to the oven for 3 to 5 minutes to heat through. Serve warm.

Stuffed Cherry Tomatoes

Preparation time: 15 minutes

Cooking time: 0 minutes

Servings: 6

Ingredients

2 pints cherry tomatoes, tops removed and centers scooped out

2 avocados, mashed

Juice of 1 lemon

½ Red bell pepper, minced

4 green onions (white and green parts), finely minced

1 tablespoon minced fresh tarragon

Pinch of sea salt

Directions:

Place the cherry tomatoes open-side up on a platter. In a small bowl, -combine the avocado, lemon juice, bell pepper, scallions, tarragon, and salt. Stir until well -combined. Scoop into the cherry tomatoes and serve immediately.

Spicy Black Bean Dip

Preparation time: 10 minutes

Cooking time: 0 minutes

Servings: 2 cups

Ingredients

1 (14-ounce) can black beans, drained and rinsed, or 1½ cups cooked

Zest and juice of 1 lime

1 tablespoon tamari, or soy sauce, ¼ Cup water

¼ Cup fresh cilantro, chopped

1 teaspoon ground cumin

Pinch cayenne pepper Directions: Put the beans in a food processor (best choice) or blender, along with the lime zest and juice, tamari, and about ¼ cup of water. Blend until smooth, then blend in the cilantro, cumin, and cayenne. If you don't have a blender or prefer a different consistency, simply transfer it to a bowl once the beans have been puréed and stir in the spices, instead of forcing the blender.

Nutrition (1 cup) calories: 190; total fat: 1g; carbs: 35g; fiber: 12g; protein: 13g

French Onion Pastry Puffs

Preparation time: 10 minutes

Cooking time: 35 minutes - makes 24 puffs

Ingredients

2 tablespoons olive oil

2 medium sweet yellow onions, thinly sliced

1 garlic clove, minced

1 teaspoon chopped fresh rosemary

Salt and freshly ground black pepper

1 tablespoon capers

1 sheet frozen vegan puff pastry, thawed

18 pitted black olives, quartered

Preparation

In a medium skillet, heat the oil over medium heat. Add the onions and garlic, season with rosemary and salt and pepper to taste. Cover and cook until very soft, stirring occasionally, about 20 minutes. Stir in the capers and set aside.

Preheat the oven to 400°f. Roll out the puff pastry and cut into 2- to 3-inch circles using a lightly floured pastry cutter or drinking glass. You should get about 2 dozen circles.

Arrange the pastry circles on baking sheets and top each with a heaping teaspoon of onion mixture, patting down to smooth the top.

Top with 3 olive quarters, arranged decoratively—either like flower petals emanating from the center or parallel to each other like 3 bars.

Bake until pastry is puffed and golden brown, about 15 minutes. Serve hot.

Cheezy Cashew–Roasted Red Pepper Toasts

Preparation time: 15 minutes

Cooking time: 0 minutes

Servings: 16 to 24 toasts

Ingredients

2 jarred roasted red peppers

1 cup unsalted cashews

1/4 cup water

1 tablespoon soy sauce

2 tablespoons chopped green onions

1/4 cup Nutritional yeast

2 tablespoons balsamic vinegar

2 tablespoons olive oil

Preparation

Use canapé or cookie cutters to cut the bread into desired shapes about 2 inches wide. If you don't have a cutter, use a knife to cut the bread into squares, triangles, or rectangles. You should get 2 to 4 pieces out of each slice of bread. Toast the bread and set aside to cool.

Coarsely chop 1 red pepper and set aside. Cut the remaining pepper into thin strips or decorative shapes and set aside for garnish.

In a blender or food processor, grind the cashews to a fine powder. Add the water and soy sauce and process until smooth. Add the chopped red pepper and puree. Add the green onions, Nutritional yeast, vinegar, and oil and process until smooth and well blended.

Spread a spoonful of the pepper mixture onto each of the toasted bread pieces and top decoratively with the reserved pepper strips. Arrange on a platter or tray and serve.

Baked Potato Chips

Preparation time: 10 minutes

Cooking time: 30 minutes

Servings: 4

Ingredients

1 large russet potato

1 teaspoon paprika

½ Teaspoon garlic salt

¼ Teaspoon vegan sugar

¼ Teaspoon onion powder

¼ Teaspoon chipotle powder or chili powder

⅛ Teaspoon salt

⅛ Teaspoon ground mustard

⅛ Teaspoon ground cayenne pepper

1 teaspoon canola oil

⅛ Teaspoon liquid smoke

Directions:

Wash and peel the potato. Cut into thin, 1/10-inch slices (a mandoline slicer or the slicer blade in a food processor is helpful for consistently sized slices).

Fill a large bowl with enough very cold water to cover the potato. Transfer the potato slices to the bowl and soak for 20 minutes.

Preheat the oven to 400°f. Line a baking sheet with parchment paper.

In a small bowl, combine the paprika, garlic salt, sugar, onion powder, chipotle powder, salt, mustard, and cayenne.

Drain and rinse the potato slices and pat dry with a paper towel.

Transfer to a large bowl.

Add the canola oil, liquid smoke, and spice mixture to the bowl. Toss to coat.

Transfer the potatoes to the Prepared baking sheet.

Bake for 15 minutes. Flip the chips over and bake for 15 minutes longer, until browned. Transfer the chips to 4 storage containers or large glass jars. Let cool before closing the lids tightly.

Nutrition: calories: 89; fat: 1g; protein: 2g; carbohydrates: 18g; fiber: 2g; sugar: 1g; sodium: 65mg

Mushrooms Stuffed With Spinach And Walnuts

Preparation time: 10 minutes

Cooking time: 6 minutes

Servings: 4 to 6 servings

Ingredients

2 tablespoons olive oil

8 ounces white mushroom, lightly rinsed, patted dry, and stems reserved

1 garlic clove, minced

1 cup cooked spinach

1 cup finely chopped walnuts

1/2 cup unseasoned dry bread crumbs

Salt and freshly ground black pepper

Preparation

Preheat the oven to 400°f. Lightly oil a large baking pan and set aside. In a large skillet, heat the oil over medium heat. Add the mushroom caps and cook for 2 minutes to soften slightly. Remove from the skillet and set aside.

Chop the mushroom stems and add to the same skillet. Add the garlic and cook over medium heat until softened, about 2 minutes. Stir in the spinach, walnuts, bread crumbs, and salt and pepper to taste. Cook for 2 minutes, stirring well to combine.

Fill the reserved mushroom caps with the stuffing mixture and arrange in the baking pan. Bake until the mushrooms are tender and the filling is hot, about 10 minutes. Serve hot.

Salsa Fresca

Preparation time: 15 minutes

Cooking time: 0 minutes

Servings: 4

Ingredients

3 large heirloom tomatoes or other fresh tomatoes, chopped

½ Red onion, finely chopped

½ Bunch cilantro, chopped

2 garlic cloves, minced

1 jalapeño, minced

Juice of 1 lime, or 1 tablespoon Prepared lime juice

¼ Cup olive oil

Sea salt

Whole-grain tortilla chips, for serving

Directions:

In a small bowl, combine the tomatoes, onion, cilantro, garlic, jalapeño, lime juice, and olive oil and mix well. Allow to sit at room temperature for 15 minutes. Season with salt.

Serve with tortilla chips.

The salsa can be stored in an airtight container in the refrigerator for up to 1 week.

64. Guacamole

Preparation time: 10 minutes

Cooking time: 0 minutes

Servings: 2

Ingredients

2 ripe avocados

2 garlic cloves, pressed

Zest and juice of 1 lime

1 teaspoon ground cumin

Pinch sea salt

Pinch freshly ground black pepper

Pinch cayenne pepper (optional)

Directions:

Mash the avocados in a large bowl. Add the rest of the Ingredients and stir to combine.

Try adding diced tomatoes (cherry are divine), chopped scallions or chives, chopped fresh cilantro or basil, lemon rather than lime, paprika, or whatever you think would taste good!

Nutrition (1 cup) calories: 258; total fat: 22g; carbs: 18g; fiber: 11g; protein: 4g

Veggie Hummus Pinwheels

Preparation time: 10 minutes

Cooking time: 0 minutes

Servings: 3

Ingredients

3 whole-grain, spinach, flour, or gluten-free tortillas

3 large swiss chard leaves

¾ Cup edamame hummus or Prepared hummus

¾ Cup shredded carrots

Directions:

Lay 1 tortilla flat on a cutting board.

Place 1 swiss chard leaf over the tortilla. Spread ¼ cup of hummus over the swiss chard. Spread ¼ cup of carrots over the hummus. Starting at one end of the tortilla, roll tightly toward the opposite side. Slice each roll up into 6 pieces. Place in a single-serving storage container. Repeat with the remaining tortillas and filling and seal the lids.

Nutrition: calories: 254; fat: 8g; protein: 10g; carbohydrates: 39g; fiber: 8g; sugar: 4g; sodium: 488mg

Asian Lettuce Rolls

Preparation time: 15 minutes

Cooking time: 5 minutes

Servings: 4

Ingredients

2 ounces rice noodles, 2 tablespoons chopped thai basil

2 tablespoons chopped cilantro

1 garlic clove, minced, 1 tablespoon minced fresh ginger

Juice of ½ lime, or 2 teaspoons Prepared lime juice

2 tablespoons soy sauce

1 cucumber, julienned

2 carrots, peeled and julienned, 8 leaves butter lettuce

Directions: Cook the rice noodles according to package Preparation. In a small bowl, whisk together the basil, cilantro, garlic, ginger, lime juice, and soy sauce. Toss with the cooked noodles, cucumber, and carrots. Divide the mixture evenly among lettuce leaves and roll. Secure with a toothpick and serve immediately.

Pinto-Pecan Fireballs

Preparation time: 5 minutes

Cooking time: 30 minutes

Servings: about 20 pieces

Ingredients

1-1/2 cups cooked or 1 (15.5-ounce) can pinto beans, drained and rinsed

1/2 cup chopped pecans

1/4 cup minced green onions

1 garlic clove, minced

3 tablespoons wheat gluten flour (vital wheat gluten)

3 tablespoons unseasoned dry bread crumbs

4 tablespoons tabasco or other hot sauce

1/4 teaspoon salt

1/8 teaspoon ground cayenne

1/4 cup vegan margarine

Preparation

Preheat the oven to 350°f. Lightly oil a 9 x 13-inch baking pan and set aside. Blot the drained beans well with a paper towel, pressing out any excess liquid. In a food processor, combine the pinto beans, pecans, green onions, garlic, flour, bread crumbs, 2 tablespoons of the tabasco, salt, and cayenne. Pulse until well combined, leaving some texture. Use your hands to roll the mixture firmly into 1-inch balls.

Place the balls in the Prepared baking pan and bake until nicely browned, about 25 to 30 minutes, turning halfway through.

Meanwhile, in small saucepan, combine the remaining 2 tablespoons tabasco and the margarine and melt over low heat. Pour the sauce over the fireballs and bake 10 minutes longer. Serve immediately.

Chapter 12.   Pre-Workout Recipes

Vegan Chili

Preparation time: 10 minutes

Cooking time: 30 minutes

Servings: 6

Calories: 340

Ingredients

2 tablespoons olive oil

3 cloves of garlic, minced

1 teaspoon chili powder

1 large red onion, thinly sliced

2 celery stalks, finely chopped

1 teaspoon ground cumin

2 medium carrots, peeled and finely chopped

2 red peppers, roughly chopped

Salt and pepper, to taste

28 ounces canned chopped tomatoes

14 ounces red kidney beans, drained and rinsed

3½ ounces split red lentils

14 ounces frozen soy mince

2 tablespoons vegetable stock

Optional:

1 teaspoon miso paste

Large handful fresh coriander, roughly chopped

2 tablespoons balsamic vinegar

To Serve:

Cooked basmati rice

A squeeze of lime juice

Extra chopped coriander

Preparation

Heat olive oil in a large saucepan.

Sauté the onion, garlic, carrot, celery, and peppers for a few minutes on medium heat, until softened.

Add the chili powder, cumin, salt, and pepper and stir.

Toss in the chopped kidney beans, tomatoes, lentils, vegetable stock, and soy mince. Add the extra flavorings, if using.

Simmer for 20 minutes.

Serve with steamed basmati rice, some fresh, torn coriander and a little squeeze of lime juice. Enjoy!

Note: Freezes well. Keep it refrigerated for up to four days.

Nutrition:

Calories 340

Total Fats 6g Saturated Fats 2g

Total Carbohydrates 42g Dietary Fiber 18g

Total Sugar 1g Protein 25g

Sweet Potato Meal Bowls

Cooking time: 25 minutes

Servings: 4

Calories: 230

Ingredients

1 large potato, diced into small pieces

3-4 tablespoons olive oil, divided

1 teaspoon seasoning of your choice(or more to taste)

Garlic powder to taste

Salt and pepper to taste

1 can sweet corn, drained

1 can black beans, drained & rinsed

Juice of ½ lime+wedges for serving

½ teaspoon ground cumin

Preparation time: 15 minutes

Preparation

Preheat your oven to 400 degrees F, move the oven rack to the top third of the oven.

Place the cubed sweet potato onto a foil-lined baking sheet. Sprinkle with the seasoning, garlic powder, and salt and pepper, and toss with two to three tablespoon of olive oil. Be sure each piece is coated in oil, but not dripping. Bake for 25 minutes or until tender.

Meanwhile, add the corn, beans, 1 tablespoon of olive oil, lime juice, cumin, salt and pepper (optional) to a small bowl. Toss.

Once your sweet potatoes are ready, equally divide them and the bean/corn mixture between the 4 containers. Add wedge of lime to each container.

Nutrition:

Calories 230 Total Fats 16g Saturated Fats 4g

Total Carbohydrates 64g Dietary Fiber 14g

Total Sugar 12g Protein 12g

Marinated Mushroom Bowls with Wild Rice and Lentils

Preparation time: 10 minutes

Cooking time: 30 minutes

Servings: 4

Calories: 285

Ingredients

Marinated Mushrooms:

¼ cup extra-virgin olive oil

2 tablespoons unseasoned rice vinegar

1 teaspoon low-sodium wheat-free tamari or soy sauce

2 teaspoon dark sesame oil

1 teaspoon chili oil

1 green onion, thinly sliced

1 tablespoon fresh cilantro, chopped

8 ounces crimini mushrooms, thinly sliced

1 teaspoon sesame seeds

Other:

2 cups thinly sliced purple cabbage

1 tablespoon fresh lime juice

Pinch of salt

2 teaspoons low-sodium soy sauce, or (for gluten free) wheat-free tamari, divided

1 cup cooked wild rice

2 cups cooked French lentils

1 cup chopped cucumber

Preparation

To marinate the mushroom, whisk the olive oil, soy sauce, rice vinegar, sesame oil, and chili oil together in a shallow bowl.

Stir in the cilantro, green onion, and sesame seeds. Add in the mushrooms and gently toss in marinade. Cover and let rest 30 minutes.

Place cabbage in a medium-sized bowl and toss with lime juice and a pinch of salt.

Stir one teaspoon of the soy sauce or tamari into the lentils and one teaspoon into the wild rice.

To serve, arrange equal parts of lentils, mushrooms, cabbage, wild rice, and cucumbers in each of the four serving bowls.

Drizzle with the remaining marinade, garnish with chopped cilantro, sliced green onions, and black sesame seeds. Serve with lime wedges.

Nutrition:

Calories 285

Total Fats 10g

Saturated Fats 2.5g

Total Carbohydrates 64g

Dietary Fiber 2g

Total Sugar 16g

Protein 19g

Chirashi Grain Bowl

Preparation time: 5 minutes

Cooking time: 15 minutes

Servings: 3

Calories: 305

Preparation:

Ingredients

7 tablespoons quinoa

4 tablespoons pearl barley

2 ounces lentils

8 broccoli florets

Handful salad leaves

Sesame salad dressing

3 ounces tofu, diced

5 tablespoons edamame, cooked

½ avocado, smashed

5 ounces pickled red cabbage,

1 carrot, thinly sliced

Miso Eggplant:

1 eggplant, diced

1 tablespoon white miso paste

1½ tablespoons mirin

2 teaspoons sugar, 2 teaspoons soy sauce

This protein packed meal with lentils, tofu, quinoa, and edamame combine to offer a full spread of muscle-building amino acids. In a small skillet, sauté the eggplant. Add the mirin, miso, soy sauce, sugar, and a dash of water. Simmer together until soft. Cook grains and the lentils according to the Preparation on the package. Steam broccoli–or any high-protein vegetables of your choice. Dress the leaves and grains and fill a serving bowl. Top with tofu, vegetables, and beans, including one spoonful of the eggplant, arranged in a circle–this is the "chirashi" style. Enjoy it with your chopsticks or fork

Nutrition: Calories 305

Total Fats 14g Saturated Fats 3g Total Carbohydrates 35g

Dietary Fiber 15g Total Sugar 5g Protein 33g

Mushroom Spinach Tofu Wraps

Preparation time: 20 minutes

Cooking time: 20 minutes

Servings: 1

Calories: 305

Ingredients

Cilantro Hummus:

1 14-ounce can chickpeas, rinsed and drained

1 tablespoon tahini

¾ teaspoons salt

1 teaspoon olive oil

Lemon juice of half a lemon

1 tablespoon water+more to thin out

4 stalks of cilantro

Mushroom Pecan Burgers

Preparation time: 15 minutes

Cooking time: 20 minutes

Servings: 5

Ingredients

9 ounces portobello mushrooms

¼ cup red onion, diced

2 cloves garlic, chopped fine or minced

1 cup pecans, diced small

1 15-ounce can chickpeas, drained and patted dry

2 cups instant oats

2 tablespoons hoisin sauce

1 tablespoon tahini or almond butter

Calories: 285

Preparation

Add 2 tablespoons of water to a large skillet. Raise heat to medium high, add the sliced portobello mushrooms. Sauté for 5 minutes.

Add in the onion and sauté for another 5 minutes. Add the garlic and cook 2 more minutes.

Remove from heat, add to a food processor with the pecans and chickpeas. Add the oats (only if they are rolled and not instant).

Process with few pulses to get all the ingredients into small pieces, no chunks.

Transfer to a large mixing bowl and add the tahini and hoisin sauce. If you're using instant oats add that now too.

Mix well. You can also use your hands and work it to work it together well.

Form into 6 patties. You can press them into a round form such as an English Muffin tin round or a pancake ring, about three inches across.

Fry in oil on one side until crispy browned, then carefully flip and brown on the other side.

Serve!

Note: You can also serve these delicious patties on a whole wheat buns with some hoisin sauce on the bottom buns and some vegan mayo on the patty. You can add curly greens and slices of red onion.

Nutrition:

Calories 285

Total Fats 18g

Saturated Fats 1g

Total Carbohydrates 30g

Dietary Fiber 8g

Total Sugar 8g

Protein 13g

Healthy Vegan Tempeh

Preparation time: 30 minutes

Cooking time: 10 minutes

Servings: 2

Calories: 574

Ingredients

Marinated Tempeh:

8 ounces 1 package tempeh

½ cup vegetable broth

1 tablespoon balsamic vinegar

1 tablespoon vegan Worcestershire sauce

1 teaspoon liquid smoke

1 teaspoon onion powder

1 teaspoon smoked paprika

½ teaspoon garlic powder

Other:

4 slices Alvarado's Sprouted Rye Seed Bread

½ heaping cup sauerkraut

¼ cup vegan Russian dressing

Vegan swiss cheese optional

2 tablespoons oil

1 tablespoon vegan butter

Preparation

Slice tempeh in half lengthwise, then slice through the middle into four thin slices.

Combine all the ingredients for the tempeh marinade in a shallow dish. Add the tempeh and marinate for at least 30 minutes.

Heat a large cast-iron skillet on medium heat with two tablespoons oil. Add the tempeh and cook for about 5 minutes per side, until it's dark brown. Once both sides are well-browned, add reserved marinade and allow it to cook off in the skillet. This enables the flavors to seep deeper into the tempeh.

Butter four slices of Sprouted Rye Seed Bread. Place on the skillet and cook for 3-4 minutes, until lightly brown. Flip the bread. On the uncooked sides, add Russian dressing to all slices of bread. Divide the sauerkraut between two slices, top with two pieces cooked tempeh each and one slice of vegan swiss, if using. Add the second slice of bread, cook on each side for about 5 minutes, until the bread is browned and everything is evenly-cooked all the way through.

Remove from the heat and serve immediately.

Nutrition:

Calories 574

Total Fats 33g

Saturated Fats 5g

Total Carbohydrates 47g

Dietary Fiber 4g

Total Sugar 5g

Protein 26g

Broccoli Pesto with Pasta and Cherry Tomatoes

Preparation time: 5 minutes

Cooking time: -20 minutes

Servings: 2

Calories: 239

Ingredients

Broccoli Pesto:

½ cup walnuts

2 heaped cups broccoli florets, cooked

3 tablespoons nutritional yeast

2 cloves of garlic

3 tablespoons olive oil

Black pepper

Salt

½ cup parsley, roughly chopped

Pasta:

1 cup cherry tomatoes, sliced into halves

9 ounces whole-wheat pasta, cooked per the Preparation on the package

1 cup cooked broccoli florets

Preparation

To make the pesto, combine the ingredients in the bowl of a food processor. Season with salt and pepper. Store in one airtight container in refrigerator for up to a week.

Serve with the whole wheat pasta and cherry tomatoes. You can also add more cooked broccoli.

Nutrition:

Calories 239

Total Fats 12g

Saturated Fats 5g

Total Carbohydrates 28g

Dietary Fiber 11g

Total Sugar 9g

Protein 21g

Mongolian Meatless Beef

Preparation time: 10 minutes

Cooking time: 20 minutes

Servings: 6

Calories: 324

Ingredients

Mongolian Sauce:

2 teaspoons vegetable oil (grapeseed oil recommended)

⅓ teaspoon red pepper flakes

½ teaspoon minced or grated ginger

3 cloves minced or grated garlic

2 teaspoons cornstarch

⅓ teaspoon Chinese five spice (optional)

½ cup low-sodium soy sauce

½ cup+2 tablespoons coconut sugar (or use a scant ½ cup brown sugar)

2 tablespoons cold water

Crisped Seitan:

1½ tablespoons vegetable oil

1 pound homemade(or store-bought) seitan, cut into 1-inch pieces

Garnish:

Sliced scallions (optional)

Toasted sesame seeds (optional)

Preparation

Sauce:

Heat the vegetable oil in small saucepan over medium heat. Add ginger and garlic, stirring constantly. After 30 seconds, add the five spice (if using) and red pepper flakes, cook for 30-60 seconds more, until fragrant.

Add soy sauce and coconut sugar, stir well. Reduce the heat to a medium-low, let simmer until coconut sugar dissolves and it is slightly reduced, about 5-7 minutes, stirring occasionally.

Whisk cornstarch and cold water together then add it to pan and stir. Cook for 2-3 more minutes, until sauce becomes glossy and thickened slightly. Reduce heat to the lowest setting, keep simmering gently until it's ready to add to the seitan.

Seitan:

In your skillet, heat the oil over medium-high heat. Add seitan and cook, stirring frequently for 4-5 minutes or until slightly browned and crisped around edges.

Reduce heat to low and add the sauce. Stir to coat all the seitan pieces, continue cooking until sauce has adhered to the seitan. Remove from the heat and serve hot with rice and vegetables of your choice. Garnish with scallions and sesame seeds if desired.

Nutrition:

Calories 324

Total Fats 8g

Saturated Fats 1g

Total Carbohydrates 33g

Dietary Fiber 3g

Total Sugar 19g

Protein 29g

Mexican Lentil Soup

Preparation time: 15 minutes

Cooking time: 30 minutes

Servings: 4

Calories: 235

Ingredients

2 tablespoons extra virgin olive oil

1 yellow onion, diced

1 red bell pepper, diced

2 carrots, peeled and diced

2 celery stalks, diced

3 cloves garlic, minced

1 tablespoon cumin

¼ teaspoon smoked paprika

1 teaspoon oregano

2 cups diced tomatoes and the juices

2 (4-ounce) cans diced green chilies

2 cups green lentils, rinsed and picked over

8 cups vegetable broth

½ teaspoon salt

Dash hot sauce, plus more for serving (adjust to taste)

Fresh cilantro, for garnish

1 avocado, peeled, pitted, and diced

Directions:

Heat olive oil in large-sized pot over medium heat. Add carrots, onion, celery, and bell pepper. Sauté until it starts to soften, about 5 minutes. Add the garlic, paprika, cumin, and oregano and sauté another minute. Add the tomatoes, lentils, chilies, broth, and salt. Bring to simmer. Simmer with the lid tilted until the lentils are tender, about 30-40 minutes. Season to taste with salt and pepper. Serve the Mexican Lentil Soup topped with fresh avocado, cilantro, and a few dashes of hot sauce.

Nutrition: Calories 235 Total Fats 9g Saturated Fats 1g

Total Carbohydrates 32g Dietary Fiber 10g Total Sugar 13g Protein 12g

Chapter 13. Post-Workout Recipes

Farro Protein Bowl

Servings: 2

Preparation time: 10 minutes

Cooking time: 25 minutes

Ingredients:

1/2 cup farro, uncooked

4 ounces smoky tempeh strips

1 cup diced sweet potatoes

2 cups mixed greens

12 ounces cooked chickpeas

1 cup diced carrots

1/3 teaspoon ground black pepper

2/3 teaspoon salt

2 tablespoons roasted almonds

2 teaspoons olive oil, divided

1/4 cup hummus

1 1/4 cups water

4 lemon, cut into wedges

Directions:

Switch on the oven, then set it to 375 degrees F and let it preheat.

Meanwhile, take a medium bowl, place sweet potato and carrots in it, drizzle with 1 teaspoon oil, season with half of each salt and black pepper, toss until mixed and then spread the vegetables on a third of a large baking sheet.

Add chickpeas into the same bowl, drizzle with the remaining oil, season with remaining salt and black pepper, toss until well coated and spread the chickpeas on second-third of the baking sheet. Arrange tempeh strips on the remaining space of the baking sheet and then roast it, chickpeas and vegetables for 30 minutes, stirring vegetables and flipping tempeh strips halfway. Meanwhile, cook the farro beans and for this, take a medium pot, place it over medium-high heat, add farro grains in it, stir in a pinch of salt, pour in water and bring to a boil. Then cover the pot with a lid, switch heat to medium-low level and cook for 25 minutes until grains have turned soft. When farro has cooked, distribute evenly between two bowls, top with roasted tempeh, chickpeas, sweet potatoes, and hummus, sprinkle with almonds, and then serve with lemon wedges. Serve straight away.

Teriyaki Tofu with Quinoa

Servings: 4

Preparation time: 10 minutes

Cooking time: 20 minutes

Ingredients:

For the Tofu:

2 cups diced asparagus

14 ounces tofu, firm, pressed, ½-inch cubed

2 tablespoons chopped green onions

2 teaspoons red chili paste

1 tablespoon soy sauce

2 teaspoons olive oil

For the Sauce:

2 tablespoons minced garlic

2 teaspoons corn starch

1/2 tablespoon grated ginger

1/4 cup coconut sugar

1 tablespoon sesame oil

3 tablespoons soy sauce

1 ½ tablespoon rice vinegar

1/2 cup water

For Serving:

4 cups cooked quinoa

Directions: Prepare the tofu and for this, take a medium skillet pan, place it over medium-high heat, add 1 teaspoon of olive oil and when hot, add tofu pieces and then cook for 5 minutes until golden brown on all sides. Then transfer tofu pieces to a bowl, drizzle with soy sauce, toss until coated, and set aside until required. Prepare the sauce and for this, take a small bowl, place all of its ingredients in it and whisk until combined. Return skillet pan over medium-high heat, add remaining oil and when hot, add asparagus and then cook for 5 to 7 minutes until tender-crisp. Return tofu pieces into the pan, drizzle with Prepared sauce, toss until well combined, then switch heat to medium level and cook for 3 to 4 minutes until the sauce has thickened. Add green onions and red chili paste, stir until mixed, and then remove the pan from heat. Remove pan from heat, then distribute quinoa among serving bowls, top with tofu and vegetables, and serve.

Buddha Bowl

Servings: 2

Preparation time: 10 minutes

Cooking time: 20 minutes

Ingredients:

For the Bowl:

8 ounces tofu, firm, pressed,

1 ½ cups cooked quinoa

1 medium white onion, peeled, sliced

1 cup spinach

1 medium sweet potato, peeled, cubed

¼ cup shredded carrots

1 avocado, pitted, diced

1 cup cooked chickpeas

1 teaspoon minced garlic

1 teaspoon garlic powder

1 teaspoon ground black pepper

1 teaspoon salt

1 teaspoon red chili powder

2 tablespoons olive oil

1 lemon, juiced

For the Marinade:

½ teaspoon salt

1 teaspoon hot sauce

1 teaspoon paprika

2 teaspoons dried thyme

2 tablespoons olive oil

½ teaspoon sesame oil

Directions:

Switch on the oven, then set it to 400 degrees F and let it preheat.

Prepare the bowl and for this, take a small bowl, place all of its ingredients in it and then whisk until combined.

Cut tofu into ½-inch cubes, place them in a container, pour in Prepared marinade, toss until well coated, and then marinate tofu pieces for 30 minutes.

Take a large baking sheet, place onion, sweet potato and garlic in it, drizzle with 1 tablespoon oil, season with half of each black pepper and salt, toss until combined, and then bake for 20 minutes until cooked.

Prepare the chickpeas and for this, take a medium bowl, add chickpeas in it, add remaining salt and black pepper, garlic powder and chili powder and stir until combined.

Take a medium skillet pan, place it over medium heat, add remaining oil and when hot, add chickpeas in it and cook for 10 minutes until done.

Transfer chickpeas to a plate, add marinated tofu pieces in it and cook for 10 minutes per side until golden brown, set aside until required.

When vegetables have roasted, take a medium-large bowl, add tofu, quinoa, chickpeas, spinach, sweet potatoes, avocado, onion, and carrots, drizzle with lemon juice and toss until just mixed. Serve straight away.

Chinese Tofu and Broccoli

Servings: 4

Preparation time: 10 minutes

Cooking time: 20 minutes

Ingredients:

3 cups broccoli florets

14 ounces tofu, firm, pressed, ½-inch cubed

1 teaspoon minced garlic

1 teaspoon grated ginger

1 tablespoon cornstarch

2 tablespoons agave syrup

1 tablespoon rice vinegar

1 teaspoon olive oil

¼ cup of soy sauce

1 ½ teaspoons sesame oil, divided

1 tablespoon water

3 tablespoons vegetable broth

1 teaspoon toasted sesame seeds and more for serving

4 tablespoons sliced scallions

2 cups cooked white rice

Directions:

Take a large skillet pan, place it over medium-high heat, add olive oil and 1 teaspoon sesame oil, and when hot, add tofu pieces and cook for 4 minutes per side until golden brown.

When done, transfer the tofu pieces to a plate, add broccoli florets to the pan, pour in the broth, switch heat to medium-low level and cook for 5 minutes until broccoli has steamed, covering the pan.

Then switch heat to medium-high level, stir in ginger, garlic, and remaining sesame oil and cook for 1 minute.

Stir together cornstarch and water until smooth, add to the pan along with sesame seeds, vinegar, agave syrup, and soy sauce, stir until mixed and cook for 2 minutes until the sauce has thickened.

Return tofu pieces to the skillet pan, toss until well coated with the sauce and then remove the pan from heat. Distribute cooked rice among bowls, top with tofu and broccoli, sprinkle with scallion and sesame seeds and then serve.

Peanut Butter Tempeh with Rice

Servings: 4

Preparation time: 3 hours and 10 minutes

Cooking time: 30 minutes

Ingredients:

6.5 ounces brown rice, cooked

22 ounces Tempeh, 1-inch cubed

Olive oil as needed

For the Sauce:

4 teaspoons coconut sugar

2 tablespoons grated ginger

1 tablespoon minced garlic

2 tablespoons red chili sauce

4 tablespoons soy sauce

2 teaspoons rice vinegar

4 tablespoons peanut butter

6 tablespoons water

For the Cabbage:

1 lime, juiced

5 ounces purple cabbage, sliced

3 teaspoons sesame oil

2 teaspoons honey

For Garnish:

4 tablespoons chopped Green onion

Directions: Prepare the sauce and for this, take a large bowl, place all of its ingredients in it and whisk until combined. Add tempeh pieces into the peanut butter sauce, toss until well coated, then place the bowl in the refrigerator and let it marinate for a minimum of 3 hours. When tofu is almost marinated, switch on the oven, then set the temperature to 375 degrees F and let it preheat. Transfer marinated tempeh pieces to a baking sheet, spray with olive oil and then bake for 30 minutes until nicely browned and cooked, turning halfway. Meanwhile, Prepare the cabbage and for this, take a medium bowl, place all of its ingredients in it and toss until combined, set aside until required. When tempeh has baked, distribute cabbage, rice and tempeh pieces evenly among bowls, drizzle with the marinade sauce, garnish with green onions and then serve.

Soy Beans and Puy lentil Salad

Servings: 4

Preparation time: 10 minutes

Cooking time: 25 minutes

Ingredients:

For the Salad:

8 ounces of broccoli florets, chopped

1 red chili, deseeded, sliced

8 ounces of Puy lentils, uncooked

5 ounces sugar snap peas

5 ounces frozen soya bean, thawed

4 ¼ cups vegetable stock, hot

For the Dressing:

1-inch piece of ginger, grated

½ teaspoon minced garlic

1 lemon, juiced

1 tablespoon honey

3 tablespoons soy sauce

2 tablespoons sesame oil

Directions:

Take a large pot, place it over medium-high heat, pour in the stock, bring it to a boil, then add lentils and cook for 15 minutes until tender.

Drain the cooked lentils, transfer them to a large bowl and set aside until required.

Drain the pot, fill it half-full with water, bring it to a boil, then add broccoli florets and cook for 1 minute.

Add soya beans and peas, continue cooking for 1 minute, then drain these vegetables, rinse under cold water and transfer them to the bowl containing lentils.

Prepare the dressing and for this, take a small bowl, place all of its ingredients in it and whisk until combined.

Pour the dressing over lentil and vegetable mixture, add red chili, and stir until well mixed.

Serve straight away.

Tofu and Greens Stir-Fry with Cashews

Servings: 4

Preparation time: 5 minutes

Cooking time: 8 minutes

Ingredients:

5 ounces soya bean

1 bunch of spring onions, sliced

2 heads of bok choi, quartered, 1 head broccoli, cut into florets

10 ounces of marinated tofu pieces, 1 red chili, deseeded, sliced

2 teaspoons minced garlic, 1 tablespoon soy sauce

1 ½ tablespoon hoisin sauce, 1 tablespoon olive oil

1 ½ tablespoon roasted cashew

Directions: Take a large skillet pan, place it over high heat, add oil and when hot, add broccoli florets and cook for 5 minutes until tender. Stir in red chili and garlic, continue cooking for 1 minute, add soya beans, spring onions, tofu, and bok choi, and stir-fry for 3 minutes. Drizzle with soy sauce and hoisin sauce, sprinkle with nuts, cook for 1 minute until hot and then serve.

Spiced Crusted Tofu with Salad

Servings: 2

Preparation time: 10 minutes

Cooking time: 15 minutes

Ingredients:

For the Tofu:

8 ounces of tofu, firmed, pressed, 1-inch cubed

4 ounces sugar snap peas

3 kumquats, sliced

4 radishes, sliced

8 ounces broccoli florets

2 spring onions, chopped

1 tablespoon Japanese spice mix

2 tablespoons sesame seeds

½ tablespoon cornflour

1 tablespoon sesame oil

1 tablespoon olive oil

For the Dressing:

1 small shallot, diced

1 teaspoon grated ginger

1 tablespoon lime juice

1 teaspoon caster sugar

2 tablespoons soy sauce

1 tablespoon grapefruit juice

Directions: Prepare the dressing and for this, take a small bowl, place all of its ingredients in it and then stir until well combined. Prepare the tofu and for this, take a small bowl, add cornflour in it, stir in Japanese spice mix and sesame seeds, and then sprinkle this mixture on all sides of tofu pieces until evenly coated. Take a large pot, fill it half full with water, place it over high heat, bring it to a boil, then switch heat to medium level, add peas and broccoli and boil for 3 minutes until tender-crisp. While water comes to a boil, take a large skillet pan, place it over medium heat, add oil and when hot, add tofu pieces and cook for 5 minutes until nicely browned. When Vegetables have cooked to the desired level, distribute them evenly between two bowls, top with cooked tofu, and then drizzle with Prepared dressing. Top with spring onions, radishes, and kumquats and then serve.

Sprouts with Green Beans and Nuts

Servings: 4

Preparation time: 5 minutes

Cooking time: 12 minutes

Ingredients:

21 ounces Brussels sprouts, quartered

21 ounces green beans

4 tablespoons toasted pine nuts

1 lemon, juiced, zested

1 tablespoon olive oil

Directions:

Take a large pot, fill it half full with water, place it over high heat, bring it to a boil, then switch heat to medium level, add beans and sprouts, and boil for 3 minutes until tender-crisp and when done, drain the beans and sprouts. Take a large skillet pan, place it medium heat, add oil and when hot, add nuts and lemon zest and cook for 30 seconds. Then add sprouts and green beans, stir-fry them for 4 minutes, then season with black pepper and salt and drizzle with lemon juice. Remove pan from heat and then serve.

Tofu with Noodles

Servings: 2

Preparation time: 25 minutes

Cooking time: 25 minutes

Ingredients:

8 ounces of tofu, firm, pressed, 1-inch cubed

6 ounces dried soba noodles, cooked

½ of a large cucumber

¼ teaspoon salt

2 tablespoons caster sugar

2 tablespoons sesame seeds

4 tablespoons white miso paste

½ cup of rice wine vinegar

2 tablespoons maple syrup

½ cup olive oil

¼ cup of water

2 spring onions, shredded

Directions:

Prepare the noodles, and for this, use a vegetable peeler to cut ribbons from the cucumber and place them in a bowl.

Take a small saucepan, place it over medium heat, add sugar, salt, vinegar, and water, stir until combined, and cook for 5 minutes until the sugar has dissolved.

Pour this mixture over cucumber ribbons, then place the bowl in the refrigerator and leave it to pickle.

Prepare the tofu and for this, take a large skillet pan, add 1 tablespoon oil in it and when hot, add tofu pieces and cook for 7 to 10 minutes until nicely golden brown on all sides. When done, transfer the tofu pieces to a plate lined with kitchen towels and then set aside until required. Take a small bowl, add honey and miso paste in it, whisk until combined, and then brush this mixture on tofu pieces until evenly coated. When cucumber ribbons have pickles, drain them, and then rinse them well under cold water. Return the skillet pan over medium heat and when hot, add remaining oil, cucumber ribbons, remaining honey-miso mixture and 1 tablespoon of the cucumber pickling liquid and continue cooking for 3 minutes until warm. When done, divide soba noodles between bowls, then top evenly with tofu and cucumber ribbons, sprinkle with green onions, and then serve.

Black Bean and Seitan Stir-Fry

Servings: 4

Preparation time: 15 minutes

Cooking time: 25 minutes

Ingredients:

For the Sauce:

1 red chili, chopped

12 ounces cooked black beans

1 tablespoon minced garlic

1 teaspoon Chinese five-spice powder

2.5 ounces brown sugar

2 tablespoons rice vinegar

2 tablespoons soy sauce

1 tablespoon peanut butter

¼ cup of water

For the Stir-Fry:

12 ounces marinated seitan pieces

2 spring onions, sliced

10 ounces bok choi, chopped

1 red pepper, sliced

1 tablespoon cornflour

3 tablespoons olive oil

2 cups cooked brown rice

Directions:

Prepare the sauce, and for this, place half of the black beans in a food processor, then add remaining ingredients and pulse for 2 minutes until smooth.

Tip the sauce in a medium saucepan, place it over medium heat, cook for 5 minutes until thickened, and then set aside until required.

Drain the marinated seitan, pat dries the seitan pieces with kitchen towels, then dredge seitan into cornflour and set aside until required.

Take a large skillet pan, place it over high heat, add 1 teaspoon oil and when hot, add seitan pieces and fry them for 5 minutes until edges have turned golden brown.

When done, transfer seitan pieces to a plate and set aside until required.

Add 1 teaspoon oil into the skillet pan, add shallots, cook for 4 minutes until softened, then add red pepper, spring onion, bok choi, and remaining black beans, stir until mixed and cook for 4 minutes.

Return seitan pieces into the pan, pour in the Prepared sauce, toss until mixed, and cook for 1 minute until hot.

Serve seitan and vegetables over brown rice.

Conclusion

"The latest suggestions explain not exactly what number of grams of protein you ought to eat, yet in addition how those grams are beat for the duration of the day," Pojednic says.

"Researchers are thinking now that there's just a specific measure of protein your muscles can take-up and use in one sitting. On the off chance that you flood your framework with amino acids, sooner or later they're somewhat squandered."

Intend to get 0.25 and 0.4 grams of protein per kilogram of body weight per feast. Or on the other hand, to place it way less difficult, space out your protein more than 3 or 4 dinners per day, not only at the same time in a uber smoothie.

The other science-sponsored tip is to ensure you're eating 20-30 grams of protein inside 30 minutes (as long as an hour is presumably fine) of Preparation. " The science is somewhat muddier for eating previously and during Preparation. Pojednic says to go with your inclination, and how much nourishment you need in your stomach related tract while you're doing overwhelming squats. Over-burdening your G.I. framework is especially simple for veggie lovers, whose nourishments contain such a lot of fiber. You can get a belly throb from eating a serving of mixed greens before Preparation, on the grounds that all the blood is "shunted away" from your stomach related organs for, state, your quads. On the off chance that you would prefer not to eat before Preparation, yet need to ensure you have enough sugar in your framework to capitalize on your exercise, Pojednic suggests organic product juice.

Be that as it may, the most urgent parts of picking up muscle have nothing to do with being veggie lover.

It's not tied in with getting enough amino acids. You must eat enough calories to increase mass, and you must train hard. Farris, who went plant-situated in November 2014 (between Olympics appearances), is a world-class competitor who happens to be veggie lover—and he doesn't follow his protein by any stretch of the imagination. All things considered, he had the option to "make a few additions and, all the more critically, remain solid." He says a vegetarian diet has let him recoup quicker. "On the off chance that you can do that, you can accomplish more work. You can pummel your body more. Essentially, simply train."

(It's important that piece of the explanation Farris had no second thoughts about changing his eating routine while in a high purpose of his profession was on the grounds that he spent his prime lifting years (19-22) picking up quality without solid access to any kind of nourishment whatsoever. "In the event that I could lift and do everything when I didn't approach customary dinners, how was I going to get more fragile eating enough nourishment however changing out the fixings?")

"A major issue for vegetarians is that they can without much of a stretch under eat," Zinchenko says. "Particularly dynamic individuals who eat a great deal of entire nourishments. Without calories, your body can't make muscle."

"The primary concern is high-volume weight Preparation and getting satisfactory supplements," David says. "That is it. There are no alternate ways. The harder you hit it, the more you feed it, the more it will develop." (I accept we were discussing butts now in the discussion.)

"Clearly diet is going to give you that minor push toward the end, yet the Preparation and the commitment is actually what's going issue in the long haul for significant level competitors," Polojic says.

Goodness, and for what it's worth, we painfully need more research on veggie lovers. "Indeed, even the investigations that analyze veggie lover protein powders are not done on vegetarians," Zinchenko says. "In the event that there is someone who might want to give cash to contemplate veggie lover muscle development, I would be glad to run the investigation."

The generalization of the powerless, thin veggie lover has become so all inclusive that the vast majority would make some hard memories accepting any individual of noteworthy size or quality didn't eat meat or other creature items. This is on the grounds that we've been adapted to accept that you have to eat bunches of creature protein to assemble muscle and quality, and that protein extremely just originates from creature nourishments.

Obviously just one of those two convictions is in reality valid, as any individual who has ever observed a (herbivorous) silverback gorilla can without much of a stretch derive.

The vast majority, notwithstanding, assume athlete sare progressively similar to lions, requiring meat or some type of creature protein at each dinner to get large and solid. As talked about in What About Protein? there are numerous purposes behind how this fantasy turned out to be so imbued in the mainstream society, yet actually from the flower child culture of the 60s until decently as of late, a great deal of the individuals who followed a plant-based eating regimen were really thin. This is halfway in light of the fact that, for a very long while, a great many athletes who picked meat/creature free eating regimens did so exclusively for moral, ecological or wellbeing reasons, and didn't generally think about having large muscles. Furthermore, the individuals who cared frequently did not have the fundamental healthful understanding important to assemble muscle and quality eating plants.

As confirm in The Game Changers, the entirety of that has changed. The age of the frail, celery-crunching vegetarian is finished. Indeed, even Arnold Schwarzenegger — the back up parent of muscle and quality — is presently encouraging individuals to "simply chill it with the meat", recognizing that there is no motivation behind why eating a plant-based eating regimen should represent any boundaries to getting enormous and solid, and that doing so may much offer some noteworthy focal points.

Building muscle and quality is in reality quite basic from a physiological perspective: turn out reliably and eat heaps of nourishment. On the off chance that you train hard however don't eat enough — or eat loads of nourishment yet don't Prepare enough — you most likely won't increase a lot of muscle or get a lot more grounded. This applies to everybody, regardless of whether you eat meat or not.

For amateur lifters, eating "bunches of nourishment" signifies devouring 10-20% a larger number of calories than required for every day upkeep, and for further developed lifters, 5-10% progressively.

An incredible aspect regarding plant-based nourishment is that, by volume, it normally contains less calories than creature-based food sources, enabling us to eat increasingly all out nourishment and feel more full, without essentially increasing more muscle versus fat. You can discover increasingly about that in Getting and Staying Lean. For individuals whose top need is to pick up muscle and quality, individuals on a plant-put together eating regimen need to center with respect to plant-based nourishments that have higher caloric thickness than state, lettuce. As a rule, this implies ensuring that suppers and bites incorporate heavy measures of grains, beans, tofu and tempeh, meat and dairy choices, nuts and nut spreads, seeds, avocados, dried natural product, and so on., notwithstanding leafy foods. Those less worried about eating essentially entire nourishments can likewise incorporate plant-based meats, plant-based protein powders, plant-based protein/vitality bars — whatever it takes to get hit the fundamental caloric excess.